Le Roi s'amuse / The Prince's Play

Tony Harrison was born in Leeds in 1937. His volumes of poetry include *The Loiners* (winner of the Geoffrey Faber Memorial Prize), *Continuous, v.* (broadcast on Channel 4 in 1987, winning the Royal Television Society Award) and *The Gaze of the Gorgon* (winner of the Whitbread Prize for Poetry). Recognized as Britain's leading theatre and film poet, Tony Harrison has written extensively for the National Theatre, the New York Metropolitan Opera, the BBC, Channel 4, and for unique ancient spaces in Greece and Austria. His *Theatre Works 1973–1985* are published by Penguin and his theatre works *The Trackers of Oxyrhynchus, Square Round, The Common Chorus, The Mysteries* and *Tony Harrison: Plays Three (Poetry or Bust, The Kaisers of Carnuntum, The Labourers of Herakles)* by Faber and Faber. His film *Black Daisies for the Bride* won the Prix Italia in 1994; this and his volume of film/poems *The Shadow of Hiroshima and other film/poems* are published by Faber and Faber.

by the same author

poetry
THE LOINERS
PALLADAS: POEMS
FROM THE SCHOOL OF ELOQUENCE
CONTINUOUS
V.
SELECTED POEMS
A COLD COMING
PERMANENTLY BARD

plays
THE MYSTERIES
THE TRACKERS OF OXYRYNCHUS
THE COMMON CHORUS
SQUARE ROUNDS
THEATRE WORKS 1975–1985
TONY HARRISON: PLAYS THREE
(POETRY OR BUST, THE KAISERS OF CARNUNTUM,
THE LABOURERS OF HERAKLES)

film/poems
BLACK DAISIES FOR THE BRIDE
THE SHADOW OF HIROSHIMA AND OTHER FILM/POEMS
(A MAYBE DAY IN KAZAKHSTAN, THE GAZE OF THE GORGON,
THE BLASPHEMER'S BANQUET, LOVING MEMORY)

VICTOR HUGO / TONY HARRISON

Le Roi s'amuse / The Prince's Play

faber and faber
LONDON · BOSTON

1996

First published in 1996
by Faber and Faber Limited
3 Queen Square London WC1N 3AU

Typeset by Faber and Faber Ltd
Printed in England by Clays Ltd, St Ives plc

© Tony Harrison, 1996

Tony Harrison is hereby identified as author of this
work in accordance with Section 77 of the Copyright,
Designs and Patents Act 1988

A CIP record for this book
is available from the British Library

ISBN 0–571–17965–7

2 4 6 8 10 9 7 5 3 1

The Prince's Play was first performed in the Olivier
Theatre at the Royal National Theatre on 19 April with
the following company:

Scotty Scott, the Comic Ken Stott
HRH The Prince of Wales David Westhead
Barmaid Catherine Tate
Lord Tourland Andrew Havill
Lord Gordon William Chubb
Lady Gossett Michele Moran
Lord Gossett Robert Swann
Lady Coslin Kathleen McGoldrick
The Poet Laureate Iain Mitchell
The Duke of Peen Joseph Bennett
Sir Percival Dillon Dugald Bruce-Lockhart
Montgomery Martin Chamberlain
Lord Bryan Simon Markey
Waiter at the Café Royal Thierry Harcourt
Lord Kintyre Michael Bryant
The Diddicoy Sean Chapman
Equerry Patrick Baladi
HRH's Bodyguard Anthony Renshaw
Becky, the Comic's daughter Arlene Cockburn
Mrs Bryden June Watson
Magdalena Rachel Power
Woman Judith Coke
Carter Edward Clayton
Doctor Paul Benzing

Other parts played by members of the company.

Director Richard Eyre
Designer Bob Crowley
Lighting Jean Kalman
Music Richard Blackford
Director of Movement Jane Gibson
Dialect Coach Joan Washington
Sound Paul Groothuis
Stage Manager Trish Montemuro
Deputy Stage Manager Fiona Bardsley
Assistant Stage Managers Valerie Fox, Andrew Speed

Grateful thanks are due to Marion Holland
for invaluable assistance with research.
T. H.

Act One: Lord Kintyre

SCENE ONE

*We hear the sound of someone being followed in a cob-
bled street. The sound intensifies to the sound of dancing
clogs which are then seen dancing in a narrow circle of
spotlight. The spotlight widens to reveal The Comic
(Scotty Scott) dressed as a woman doing a clog dance in a
London Music Hall with a golden proscenium.*

  *HRH The Prince of Wales with various aristocratic
hangers-on is in a box near the stage. The act ends. Scotty
Scott curtsies to the 'royal box'. HRH throws him a bouquet which Scotty Scott picks up and clasps to his bosom
and curtsies again.*

  *Exit Scotty Scott to change for the next number. It is
the interval. A Barmaid brings in champagne and glasses
for HRH's party. HRH gooses the Barmaid as she pours
his champagne.*

Barmaid
Your Royal Highness!

(*Exit Barmaid.*)

HRH
              Fillies, eh? And fizz!
Is there more to life? Don't think there is.
Fillies and fizz! What else is there beside?
And I've found a filly I can't wait to ride.
Nothing like the hunt! My sights are set
on game I haven't had much luck with yet,
but I won't be happy till she's in my snare.
An obvious pleb, of course, born God knows where,
but so damnably enticing!

Lord Tourland
Is it her
you've followed to chapel these past Sundays, sir?

HRH
(*laughing*)

A Cheapside chapel! Praying in my pew!

Lord Tourland
You've been up to this at least a month or two.

HRH
I know.

Lord Tourland
And she lives where, this present belle?

HRH
Close to Lord Gossett's.

Lord Tourland
Gossett's, know it well.
Splendid mansion! Somewhat spoiled by views
over a rather squalid little mews.

HRH
That's Bussy Street, that unlit cul-de-sac.

Lord Tourland
Ah, so that's where you've tracked your quarry back.
Have you had the chance to get inside?

HRH
No, not at all, although I've really tried.
There's some old Scottish crone

who guards her day and night as chaperone
All she's allowed to say, to see, to hear
's decided by this dragon overseer.
But they've all got their price. I might just grease
the door ajar with a 'wee bag of bawbees'.

There's this dragon and at night a shape,
wrapped and muffled in an ink-black cape
which makes him merge with shadows, goes inside.

Lord Tourland
If he does, why can't you?

HRH
     God knows I've tried!
I'd love to get inside. I've tried to, but
the door's immediately closed fast and bolted shut.

Lord Tourland
And has this filly given your Highness cause
to think she welcomes this pursuit of yours?

HRH
Not uninterested 's my frank surmise.
No obvious revulsion in her eyes.

Lord Tourland
Is she aware that she's a prince's prey?

HRH
No, wouldn't do to give the game away.
I cultivate the homespun studious looks
of a poor student who spends his life with books.
Sallow, skinny, studious, and skint.

Lord Tourland
Probably some Bishop's secret bint!

(*A roll of drums and from behind the curtain the skirl of bagpipes being played. The curtain rises revealing Scotty Scott in full Scottish tartan, kilt and sporran, playing the bagpipes.*)

HRH

(*calling out to Scotty Scott on the stage*)

>Give us a wise ruling from the boards
>on how the ladies should be handled by these Lords.

>Silence is the secret. My advice on this is:
>seal your lips if you seek stolen kisses
>What's your opinion? Am I right or wrong!

Scotty Scott
Right, your Highness. But listen to my song.

(*Music. Scotty Scott goes into his routine song of 'The Ladies! The Ladies!'*)

Scotty Scott
(*singing*)

>Pity this poor Glasgow lad
>come to London in his plaid.
>The Ladies can't stand my pipes' lilt
>and when I sport my sporran
>they spurn me as foreign
>and I've never once lifted my kilt.

>My tartan tirade is
>the Ladies, the Ladies,
>the Ladies I love just won't stay.
>The Ladies, God bless 'em,
>I long to possess 'em

4

but Ladies, they all fly away.

The Ladies, God bless 'em,
we long to possess 'em
but Ladies, they all fly away.

The Ladies, God bless 'em,
we long to possess 'em
but Ladies, they all fly away.

Where the soldiers parade is
where you'll see the Ladies
watching fine soldiers on show,
but when stout lads present
(you know what is meant!)
the Ladies, the Ladies they always say NO!

BUT . . .

There's a lad with more luck in
these matters of . . . [friendship]
one groomed for a very posh job,
phenomenally firm in fine ermine
he's known as the nation's top nob!

(*HRH and his Troupe join in on 'top nob'.*)

The Ladies, God bless 'em
we long to possess 'em
but Ladies, they all fly away.

The Ladies, God bless 'em
we long to possess 'em
but Ladies, they all fly away.

The Ladies, the Ladies
the one who's got it made is
the man who can love 'em then flee
and there's said to be royals
who don't have the toils

and troubles the Ladies, the Ladies give me!

The dancer, the Duchess
och, all that he touches
whatever the Lady, och aye,
the Wizard of Windsor's wand wins her
he never, like Scotty, need sigh . . .

The Ladies, God bless 'em
I long to possess 'em,
but Ladies, they all fly away.

(*Scotty Scott invites the N.T. audience and Aristocrats to
engage in a singing competition using some of the following couplets.*)

1)
You in the cheap seats, let's hear you outsing
this choir of cronies of your future King!

2)
Your Royal Highness and your noble train
versus the plebs in singing my refrain:

(*If the N.T. audience does seem louder than the
Aristocrats then Scotty says:*)

1)
Your Royal Highness, your team's below par
they need a shot of champers from the bar!

2)
Your Royal Highness, your Dukes and Lords
need more *Veuve Cliquot* on their vocal cords.
Give 'em a gargle and let's see
if they can't sing my song with more *esprit*.

(*If the N.T. audience fails to respond to Scotty's cajoling,
HRH should address his subjects as follows:*)

1)
I hereby command you as your future King
to pull your fingers out at once, and sing.

2)
All our future subjects now before us
are forthwith commanded to join in the chorus.

Scotty Scott

The Ladies, God bless 'em
We long to possess 'em,
but Ladies, they all fly away.

The Ladies, the Ladies
the one time I strayed is
the time when the wife was away.
But the wife came back early
caught me and my girly
dreadf'ly indecorous and *déshabillé*!

Och, I know what the French is
for wenches, for wenches,
the wenches in French are all *filles*
No *fille* ever winces at princes
but wenches all wince to meet me.

The Ladies, God bless 'em
I long to possess 'em,
but Ladies, they all fly away.

The Ladies, God bless 'em
We long to possess 'em,
but Ladies, they all fly away

The Ladies, the Ladies,
one Lady who stayed is
one that I wished had took flight.
and O God Almighty,
the wife in her nighty

7

will make sure I'm in bed tonight.

(*Applause and the curtain comes down, the audience exit.*)

SCENE TWO

Backstage of the same Music Hall, with dressing rooms in a long corridor with fans and aristocratic stage-door Johnnies lining the walls waiting for chorus girls etc.
HRH and retinue are loitering about watching the women pass, straining to catch a glimpse of stocking in the women's dressing rooms.

Lord Tourland
I'd love her in my bed. She's so divine.

Lord Gordon
Either of that pair would do for mine.

HRH

(*calling over to the Lords*)

Gorgeous Lady Gossett's got my choice!

Lord Gordon

(*indicating Lord Gossett, one of the fattest men in England*)

The husband's over there, sir, watch your voice!

HRH
The husband, for all I care, can go to hell.

(*HRH pursues Lady Gossett. Lord Gordon talks to Scotty Scott.*)

Lord Gordon
Wasn't Lord Kintyre's daughter this month's belle?
Seems there's a new one now. Who'd think he'd tire
so quickly of the daughter of Kintyre?
She dropped her pantaloons to save her pater
only to get the push off three weeks later.

Scotty Scott
Yes, now she's pretty shattered and heart-broken.
He hasn't written to her, hasn't spoken
for at least a week . . .

Lord Gordon
            Perhaps he'll pack
her off to her husband if he'll have her back.
After all she's paid the Prince the dues
no daughter in her place could well refuse
when he lent his influence to sway the Bar
and get her father off.

Scotty Scott
            All most bizarre.
But what possessed Kintyre to have her wed,
to pack off a beauty like her to the bed
of that bloated Birmingham Lord Mayor?

Lord Gordon
Lord Kintyre's odd! I followed the affair
and for the whole duration sat in court.
Not knowing his acquittal had been bought
for a price his precious daughter had to pay
the Prince in kind, I heard Kintyre pray
to God to bless the Prince of Wales, his friend.
Now, apparently, he's really round the bend.

HRH

(*passing with Lady Gossett*)

Leaving London? You'll tear my heart in two!

Lady Gossett

My husband's adamant, what can I do?

HRH

What can you do? I beg you, just say no.
The whole of London cries 'Don't go! Don't go!'
The name most often on the poets' lips,
most toasted by lieutenants, is your Ladyship's.
You make the city glow. You shine so bright
your leaving will plunge London into night.
You'd scorn your future monarch, scorn
the devotion of the best and noblest born,
the meteors of the metropolitan Heaven
to be a dazzling star in darkest Devon!

Lady Gossett

(*with one eye on her watching husband*)

Your Highness, sshhh!

HRH

London with you not here 's
like a ballroom when the brightest chandelier 's
been snuffed, or bright stars leave the skies.

Lady Gossett

(*pulling away from HRH as her husband approaches*)

My husband's watching us.

HRH
> O damn his eyes!

(*Lord Gossett shepherds his wife away.*)

HRH

(*to Comic*)

> I wrote that idiot's wife a passionate ode.
> It's odd our new Poet Laureate never showed
> my little effort to you.

Scotty Scott
> God forbid!
> Frankly I'm relieved he never did.
> I can't stand verses. His are bad enough
> without your Highness churning out the stuff.
> Let the Laureate make the verses, you make love.
> Only poets rhyme carnality with dove.

HRH
> Rhyming for women lifts the heart. It sings.
> It gives my royal dungeon soaring wings.

Scotty Scott
> Makes Windsor like a windmill! Then you'd find
> you did nothing else all night and day but grind!

(*For a moment HRH is offended. Scotty Scott's gone too far.*)

HRH
> I think that you've just earned a dose of whip . . .

(*HRH sees Lady Coslin passing by and says loud enough for her to hear*)

> if I weren't enamoured of her Ladyship.

Scotty Scott

(bitter from the whipping threat)

> Fickle as the wind! The feller flirts
> with everything that flounces by in skirts.

(Lord Gordon comes up to Scotty Scott.)

Lord Gordon
Watch Lady Gossett. I think we'll get
the old dropped glove routine now. Want to bet?

(Scotty Scott nods and he and Lord Gordon watch Lady Gossett as she drops her bouquet. HRH leaves Lady Coslin who he has been flirting with and retrieves the dropped bouquet, and begins to chat to Lady Gossett.)

Lord Gordon
What did I tell you? Trapped and no escape.

Scotty Scott
The ladies, they're demons in human shape.

Lord Gordon

(noticing the husband of Lady Gossett approaching)

> The husband!

Lady Gossett

(also noticing her husband)

> Your Highness, please! No more!

Scotty Scott
What's old jealous fat-guts come here for?
Old Lord Fatso's wobbling wattles all aquiver
because he sees his wife and *who* is wiv 'er!

Lord Gossett
Are they whispering about me over there?

Lord Tourland
She's very beautiful, your wife. Take care!

(*Lord Gossett backs away.*)

Lord Gordon
Why are you always so preoccupied,
continually glancing from side to side?

(*Lord Gossett backs away from Lord Gordon and finds
himself face to face with Scotty Scott.*)

Scotty Scott
It's the pressure of perpetual suspicion
that gives such mad persistence to his mission.

(*Lord Gossett bustles his wife away from HRH who
returns to his cronies.*)

HRH

(*to Scotty Scott*)

The Ladies, the Ladies! Eh, my friend!
My Heaven 's the Ladies laid end to end.
What about you?

Scotty Scott
Me, I'm the sort of bloke
who's been made to feel that life's just one big joke.
You gallivant, I glower, you cavort, I crack
the black jokes of the scathing, scorned hunchback.
Balls and sports and love affairs are best
when seen, with due detachment, as a jest.

HRH
I bless the day Her Majesty the Queen

conceived me. With Lord Gossett off the scene
I'd be ecstatic. What's your view of him?

Scotty Scott
Not only a deformity but dim!

HRH
Indisputably a dampener! His jealous bile
has rather cramped the roving royal style.
I can want what I want, and what I want I get
except for Lord Gossett's wife who's not mine, yet.
But how wonderful it is just to exist!
The world's so happy!

Scotty Scott
And the Prince so pissed!

(*HRH and Scotty Scott watch Lady Gossett, chaperoned
closely by her anxious husband.*)

HRH
Her eyes! Her arms! How beautiful she is!

(*then to Scotty Scott, leaning on him*)

Escort us to more fillies and more fizz.

(*Scotty Scott supports the tipsy HRH and they sing, as
they exit to the Café Royal, a few choruses of 'The
Ladies! The Ladies!'*)

SCENE THREE

The Café Royal. The same mixture of nobles and notables.

Poet Laureate
What's the news?

14

Lord Gordon
His Royal Highness is at play.

Poet Laureate
That's not news. It happens every day.

Lord Gossett
(*restlessly pacing the room*)

It's very bad news for some. The Prince's sport
's fine for the catcher, less fine for the caught.

Lord Gordon
Poor fat Lord Gossett makes my spirit wince.

Poet Laureate
His wife's the latest plaything of the Prince.

Lord Gordon
Ah, here's the Duke!

(*enter the* **Duke of Peen**)

Duke of Peen
(*excited, breathless*)

You'll die! You'll die!
It's something you'll be flabbergasted by.
It's sensational, hilarious, sublime.
It craves the permanence of verse and rhyme.
It needs immortalizing. A limerick
from the Laureate here would do the trick.

Poet Laureate
(*haughty and offended*)

I don't do limericks.

Duke of Peen
Oh what a toffee-nose!
You'll wish you did write limericks when I expose
the hunchback's little secret!

Sir Percival Dillon
He's lost his hunch!

Poet Laureate
They're going to serve his body up for lunch,
his head on a platter, as befits a boar,
and a great big apple jammed into his jaw.

Duke of Peen
No, nothing like that, no, the hunchback's got . . .

Montgomery
The pox!

Lord Bryan
A secret hoard of money.

Sir Percival Dillon
Not . . .
no, *not* a knighthood. That would be obscene.
I'd have to return *my* knighthood to the Queen.

Duke of Peen
No, you won't believe it. Your sides will split . . .
The hunchback 's got himself a fancy bit!

All

(*laughing*)

No! Never! Get away!

Duke of Peen
                        No, honestly, I swear.
He keeps her hidden and I've found out where.
Got her installed in grubby Bussy Street
pretty dilapidated but at least discreet.
He goes there every night wrapped in a cloak
and not looking like a man who likes a joke,
sombre and intense, more like a poet,
and nobody would ever even know it,
if I hadn't been myself . . . out for a stroll . . .
I've got a little plan. Don't tell a soul.

Poet Laureate
Yes, only a limerick could include
the paradox of him and love. I'll make it rude.

(*Lord Tourland joins them.*)

Sir Percival Dillon
Talking of dark ladies what about the Prince
who started prowling too some eight weeks since?
Like someone searching for a buried treasure.

Montgomery
What's he up to?

Lord Tourland
                        The pursuit of pleasure.
You know how it always is with him –
the wind blows and he gets a sudden whim,
this time to go about dressed in the kind
of clothes that keep him out of sight and out of mind
until he's in some bedroom, God knows whose.
But I'm not married. I've no wife to lose.

Lord Gossett
It's a very old established royal habit

to see happiness in others and then grab it.
Those I feel sorry for, the men I pity
have daughters, wives and sisters in this city
to fall ready victims to the roving eye
of the future king they'll be dishonoured by.
Exercising royal power for power's sake 's
twice as thrilling the more waste it makes.
All his Royal Highness's great gay guffaws
just show the vicious teeth that fill his jaws.

Lord Tourland
He really fears the Prince.

Sir Percival Dillon
      His wife much less.

Poet Laureate
His fear 's engendered by her fearlessness.

Lord Gordon
I think it's the duty of a Duke or Lord
to make damn sure the Prince is never bored.

Duke of Peen
Yes, when he's bored, his boredom casts a cloud
all over Britain. So boredom's not allowed.

Sir Percival Dillon
Keep him amused by any means you know.

(*They hear HRH and Scotty Scott still singing snatches of
'The Ladies! The Ladies!'*)

Here comes the Prince with 'lover-boy' in tow.

(*Enter HRH and Scotty Scott. The nobles stand for
HRH.*)

SCENE FOUR

The same. Scotty Scott looks round the company with obvious distaste for the literati and university dons.

Scotty Scott
Too many intellectuals (so called!)
around tonight, your Highness, I'm appalled.

HRH
The family rather think a poet or prof
might profit me. Something might rub off.

Scotty Scott
Your Highness, as one less drunk than you
I've got the better judgement of the two
and as one less befuddled, with a clearer brain,
rather than intellectuals I'd entertain
diarrhoea!

HRH
                     You overstep the bounds!
Educating me for when I'm crowned 's
important.

Scotty Scott
                     You'd do better in the Zoo
than chatting to that academic crew.
or meet with the mad Mahdi in Khartoum,
or trapped with twenty bishops in one room,
or officially bound for hours to be nice to
some Flemish-speaking Belgian Burgomeister,
or talk to your ancestors in stone or bronze
than listen to those droning Oxford dons.
What has scholarship to offer when the room

reeks with the Ladies' irresistible perfume?

HRH

But, supposing, my advisors say,
(perish the thought though) that there'll come a day
when the Ladies aren't enough, that's when I'd need
to study all those books I ought to read.

Scotty Scott

If things got as bad as that I'd not prescribe
the tedious ramblings of some boring scribe.
The ailment's tragic but the cure far worse –
no more Ladies only libraries of verse.
Bad advice, your Highness, family or not.

HRH

Away with the highbrows, then. I'll dump the lot.
I suppose that I could keep some poets though

Scotty Scott

Your Royal Highness, *all* the poets should go.
You and poetry, sir, I'd say they mix
as well as the Devil and a crucifix.
I'd keep poetry as much at bay
as Satan keeps the holy water spray.

HRH

Half a dozen?

Scotty Scott

One Poet Laureate's enough!
Don't overdose on it. It's poisonous stuff.

Poet Laureate

Charming!

(aside)

> One day he'll rue that jest.

Scotty Scott
The Ladies, your Highness, and to hell with the rest!
It's the Ladies, the Ladies that light up a party,
your Highness, the Ladies, not limp *literati*!

HRH
Yes, the Ladies, the Ladies. Bookworms blight
all ladies bring us of dreams and delight.

(There is laughter from a group of three men at another table.)

HRH
Are those noble bullies making cruel fun
of my comedian?

Scotty Scott

(listening)

> No, sir, the other one.

HRH
Which other comic's been invited? Who?

Scotty Scott
The comic that they're laughing at is you.
It won't be long, they say, before you're reigning
but, in actual fact, your Highness, they're complaining
that your Royal Highness is most likely to disown
his former cronies once he's on the throne.

HRH
You see the types they are?

21

Scotty Scott
              Aye!

HRH
                        Bloody shower!
I've done everything that's in my power
to give them advancement, either a command,
or a baronetcy with a lot of land,
and that ungrateful sod's my Household Squire
but they moan and whinge and want promoting higher.
Such ingratitude!

Scotty Scott
              I'd say there still was scope
to raise them higher.

HRH
How?

Scotty Scott
              The hangman's rope!

(*The three in question have overheard the conversation as
Scotty Scott intended. The Duke of Peen addresses them.*)

Duke of Peen
Did you hear what he said, that gross buffoon?

Lord Gordon
I did.

Lord Tourland
The bastard!

Sir Percival Dillon
              We'll get even soon.
We'll get that crass comedian destroyed.

Scotty Scott

In your heart, your Highness, is there no a void?
Don't all your easy conquests make you wish
you'd more angling to do to land your fish,
some catch with real passion, but impressed
more by your person than your royal crest?

HRH

How do you know there's no one in this town
who loves me for myself, and not my crown?

Scotty Scott

Who doesn't know your rank?

HRH

                           I have a 'friend'.
She lives in a cul-de-sac in the East End.

Scotty Scott

Not a pleb?

HRH

      Why not?

Scotty Scott

                    Not plebs, sir, do beware.
Loving beneath you 's a dangerous affair.
The plebs when passionate get wild and hot.
Give them an inch of you, they'll take the lot.
Princes (and comics) should be content to bed
the wives and daughters of the better bred.

HRH

I long for Lord Gossett's wife tonight in mine.

Scotty Scott

Why not? Why not?

HRH

      All very well and fine
to say why not but how?

Scotty Scott

      Abduction, say?

HRH

And what of the husband when she's dragged away?

(*Scotty Scott draws his hand across his throat.*)

HRH

Don't do that! He can see.

Scotty Scott

      Speak to the Queen.
Pay him with promotion. Know what I mean?
Speak with her Majesty. He can get his Garter,
you get both his wife's. A gentlemanly barter!

HRH

His jealousy 's like one much lesser born's.
He'd shout out from the roof and show his horns.

Scotty Scott

Awkward customer! But if he can't be bought
there are countless ways a cuckold can be caught.
Either get him some ermine as a small reward
or get him convicted for indecency or fraud.
I'd've thought to throw this idiot in jail 's
not beyond the powerful Prince of Wales.
Your Royal Highness shouldn't find it hard
to lean on some sycophant from Scotland Yard.

Concoct some serious offence and get him life
so you can have your freedom with his wife.

(*Lord Gossett has overheard the last part of Scotty Scott's
suggestion.*)

Lord Gossett

The demon!

HRH

(*to Comic*)

You're pushing him too far!

Scotty Scott

Well, what's the point of being who you are
if you can't indulge your slightest princely whim.

Lord Gossett

(*attacking Scotty Scott with a champagne bottle*)

If I'm to hang, by God I'll swing for him.

Scotty Scott

With all your weight I think the rope would snap.

Lord Gossett

I'll see you damned!

Scotty Scott

You don't scare me, old chap
I scourge the mighty with my comic act.
I stick my neck out, but my head's intact.
All I'm afraid of 's if my hump were where
your belly is. That would make me care.
Then I'd be really ugly.

Lord Gossett
You common Glasgow bore!

HRH

(*suddenly severe*)

That's enough. From both of you. No more!

(*HRH's Bodyguard and others restrain Lord Gossett and HRH leads Scotty Scott away from the fracas.*)

Lord Gordon
HRH finds everything so droll.

Sir Percival Dillon
He laughs at anything. Got no control.

Poet Laureate
Strange for me to see our Prince at play.

Lord Bryan
That comedian. We've got to make him pay.

All
Hear, hear!

Poet Laureate
But how? It's very hard
to get at him. He's under 'Royal guard'.

Sir Percival Dillon
Notwithstanding all the people he 's offended
the vile buffoon's immune as he's befriended
by the Prince who finds the clown amusing
although it's mostly us he keeps abusing.
Everybody here 's got cause to bear
the joker grudges, but get him, how and where?

Duke of Peen
I know a way. And I suggest we meet
later on tonight in Bussy Street,
close to Lord Gossett's.

Poet Laureate
(*seeing a chance to get his own back*)

I get the idea!

All
Agreed! You're on!

Sir Percival Dillon
But sshhh! The clown might hear!

Scotty Scott
Who can I torment now, what target hit,
straight to the bullseye with my bolts of wit?

(*A Waiter approaches Scotty Scott*)

Waiter
An elderly gentleman in formal black attire
demands to see his Highness. Claims he's Lord Kintyre.

Scotty Scott
(*recognizing an opportunity for sport*)

Ah, ha! Lord Kintyre! By all means
show him in. Oh *now* we'll have some scenes!

The Voice of Lord Kintyre
(*from outside the room*)

Only his Highness! I will address
only his Royal Highness, no one less!

HRH

Who the devil 's that?

The Voice of Lord Kintyre
I will remain until
I see his Highness . . .

(*HRH recognizes the voice of one whose daughter he has
seduced and signals that he must not be let in but Lord
Kintyre bursts through the crowded room and confronts
HRH.*)

SCENE FIVE

Lord Kintyre
Speak to you I *will*!

HRH

Lord Kintyre!

Lord Kintyre
Lord Kintyre, in fact.

Scotty Scott

(*to HRH*)

Sir, let me read this gent the Riot Act!

(*turning on Lord Kintyre*)

They would have locked you up and lost the key
if his Highness hadn't schemed to get you free.
Since those delinquencies you're even dafter.
Are all of us to fall about with laughter
or look at your madness with astonished awe?

(*appealing to the crowd*)

This gent wants grandsons from . . . his son-in-law!

Sired by his son-in-law! I mean
he's the ugliest monster that I've ever seen.
Hairy, pasty, stunted and half-blind,
deformed like him in front, like me behind.
Your gorgeous daughter and your son-in-law,
conjugally speaking, make the world guffaw.
If the Prince had not seen fit to intervene
what a brood of monsters you'd have seen:
ginger-haired, gap-toothed, and gross deformity,
in front like my Lord, behind like me.
If you want grandsons with no handicap
to pull your beard and clamber on your lap,
the way to get such grandsons on your knees is
to let the Prince play how and when he pleases!

(*This final flourish causes general hoots of laughter among HRH's hangers-on.*)

Lord Kintyre

More affront! Sir, you are a prince, a title
which obliges you to hear my sad recital.
Not long ago when I was brought to trial
and, most unexpectedly, saw Fortune smile,
my foolish dream had led me to believe
the Prince of Wales had worked for my reprieve.
Bear in mind my noble forebears (mine
is an ancient, honourable line)
when I tell you, sir, I'd rather languish
in a cell till death than feel the anguish
I feel now, go to the gallows even, rather
than feel the pain I feel now as a father,
knowing, as I do, that, to clear my name
my daughter bought my honour with her shame.
Her slandered father could be soon acquitted

provided, she'd been told, that she submitted
to your callous lust that could well spread its stain
over the country, if you ever reign.
My reprieve and pardon were a Prince's plan
to drag my daughter to his soiled divan.
If we lived in an age when monarchs' power
had enemies beheaded in the Tower,
(and with fathers and husbands who obstruct your joy
you'd like the headsman's axe in your employ)
and, as one such obstruction, I myself had been
a headless innocent on Tower Green,
beheaded at your behest, I swear my ghost
would haunt you everywhere where you played host
to revellers and roués, and other royal rakes,
and, in the name of fathers, for our daughters' sakes,
the head I carried in my hands would cry:
the man my daughter was dishonoured by.
That head with bitter tongue and bloodied beard
would be the phantom that you always feared,
when ogling, or groping, guzzling, glad or gay –
my ghost would sour your every suave soirée,
still the spectre at your feasts who will proclaim
the roué prince pollutes his Royal name!

HRH

(*choking with rage*)

Have you forgotten whom you stand before?

(*to Bodyguard*)

Throw this fellow out and call the Law!

Scotty Scott
He's either barmy or been on the booze.

Lord Kintyre

I curse you both! Mock me if you choose,
but it's quite unpardonably vulgar, sir,
to have me snapped at by your mongrel cur,
like an old lion forced down to its knees
by the yapping of a pampered Pekinese.

(*turning on Scotty Scott*)

I curse you, and forecast a future hour
when your sycophantic satire will turn sour.
All this frivolous fun you're paid to poke
won't seem so funny when your fate 's the joke.
Your unfortunate but fitting malformation
puts you beyond the pale of procreation,
but if you were capable my curse would be
to know, as I did, proud paternity,
to sire, as I did, a beloved child,
who'd be, as mine was, shamefully defiled.

(*to HRH*)

Your crown is of gold, mine these hairs of white.
Both crowns should have respect and proper right.
A Prince takes his own vengeance. Mine
is in the far more powerful hands of the Divine!

Act Two: The Diddicoy

SCENE ONE

Scotty Scott
I'm bothered by it, that old fellow's curse.

The Diddicoy

(*emerging from the shadows*)

Evening, sir!

Scotty Scott

(*assuming that he's being robbed*)

I've nothing in my purse.

The Diddicoy
Who said I wanted it? You do me wrong.

Scotty Scott
Then I hope that you won't detain me long.

The Diddicoy
You're hasty in your judgement, sir, my trade
's professional services, with a blade.

Scotty Scott
A cut-throat. God!

The Diddicoy
        I've watched you every night,
restless and worried, looking left and right.
Not like I've seen you on the boards

'working the house' from humble folk to Lords,
nah, more like a nervous man whose eyes survey
every shadowy street and alleyway.
It's my guess that a Lady is the cause.

Scotty Scott
What's that to you?

The Diddicoy
       My interests are yours.
You seem like a bloke who might need to employ
the blade-craft and discretion of the Diddicoy.
Maybe some swell or blackguard 's blowing kisses
or making sheep's eyes at the missus,
you'd like seeing to?

Scotty Scott
       What are you saying?

The Diddicoy
Seeing to, assassinating, slashing, slaying!
A modest honorarium would guarantee
your missus's molester's·R.I.P.
I'm a bloke to whom the ladies can apply
to have their honours well protected by.

Scotty Scott
So what would you charge to execute a
persistent pest like an unwanted suitor?

The Diddicoy
Depends on who you're doing in. Degrees
of danger or of class adjust the fees.

Scotty Scott
So if the man's of rank?

The Diddicoy
                    Nobs cost double.
Disposing of your nobs is far more trouble.
They might have minders and so killing nobs
is riskier than ordinary jobs.
With assassination your sliding scale 's
from paupers (cheap!) to top-price Prince of Wales.

Scotty Scott

(*laughing*)

Top-price Prince of Wales! And is your blade
in much demand?

The Diddicoy
                    Never short of trade.
But hiring assassins is a hobby which
requires your hirer to be rather rich.
It's a luxury most people can't afford.
You've got to be loaded like a Duke or Lord.
Or blokes like you, sir, who have made their pile
and can affect the gentlemanly style.
Self-made men with secrets hire my skill.
Half down-payment, half after I kill.

Scotty Scott
Risky if you're caught.

The Diddicoy
                    Nah, some golden grease
works wonders on the palms of the Police.

Scotty Scott
So much a head?

The Diddicoy
Yer, but I couldn't oil
their palms enough if I'd done like, say, a Royal.

Scotty Scott
How do you go about it?

The Diddicoy
Right on the street
or back at my place.

Scotty Scott
That sounds more discreet!

The Diddicoy
My sister helps me. She's the baited trap.
She knows all the ways there are to tempt a chap.
But before he gets his wicked way, sir,
I'm in there brandishing my whistling razor.

Scotty Scott
I see.

The Diddicoy
Minimum of fuss. No noise. No stir.
I aim to give good, decent service, sir.
Give me your custom and I guarantee
you'll have full satisfaction for your fee.
I'm not a gang whose way to get things done
's to mob the man in question ten to one.
I operate alone with the discretion
best suited to a man in my profession.
I'm not your ordinary East End chivver,
those windbags who can brag but don't deliver.
Me, and my honed helper, yours to summon
to stop that feller pestering your woman.

Scotty Scott

There's no woman, so I don't require
the services you're offering for hire.

The Diddicoy

Bear me in mind. If you ever want to meet
Come to *The Fiddlers*, Lower Dorset Street.
Ask for the Diddicoy.

Scotty Scott

And join the queue!

The Diddicoy

Don't despise me.

Scotty Scott

We've both got jobs to do!

The Diddicoy

At least I give a service for my pay.
I'm not on the welfare, skiving off all day.
I've got four kids to bring up and support.

Scotty Scott

And you want to raise them as a father ought.
I wish you well.

The Diddicoy

(*holding up his razor*)

Your humble servants, sir. *Adios!*

(*Exit The Diddicoy.*)

Scotty Scott

(*watching him disappear into the night*)

The cut-throat and the comic are quite close!
He works with a well-honed razor, me,
I wound my victims with sharp repartee.

SCENE TWO

Scotty Scott

The old man damned me. Even as he spoke
and yelled his curse at me I made a joke.
I mocked him. I was my wicked self all right,
but inside my soul was shuddering with fright.
Cursed. Damned. Nature and society combined
have shaped me with a warped and grudging mind.
Comedy and crippledom have made me bitter.
I'm tired of making titled dim-wits titter.

Even in dreams when I escape
out of my world I still wake up this shape.
All I'm good for, all my life and worth
depends on moving men I loathe to mirth.
It's so humiliating. All men have the right
to shed their tears, even troops who fight
massed together round the tattered rag
they flatter with the name of national flag,
the convicts chained together who've been sent
to Australia, scorn laughter and lament.
The prisoners cooped for life in Pentonville
can break down in their cells and weep their fill.
They're captive creatures, yet they're free
to sob their hearts out fully, but not me.
All men who suffer weep, and only I,
the constant comic, have no right to cry

There's nothing in a hump to make you proud,
I burn with envy at the well-endowed.
All the surrounding sparkle and gay glitter

only makes me blacker and more bitter
I've no sooner found some corner to console
my inner anguish, and my grieving soul
when up he comes, his Highness, full of vim,
(he's powerful, he's loved by women, him)
young, handsome, Britain's noblest born,
up his Highness comes, and with a yawn
gives me a kick when I'm quite lost in grief,
and says 'Come on, I need some light relief'.

Bloody Court jester! I've a human heart
that doesn't always want to play the part.
All my dark feelings, anger, envy, rage,
all the vitriol I should fling on the age,
that boiling tar of passions in my breast,
when he clicks his fingers, gets suppressed.
One flick from the Prince of Wales's whip
I stifle my suffering, and crack a quip.
Up, down, left, right, no matter whether
I jump or run or sit I feel my tether.

Humiliation from the men 's a constant hell,
and when I think I might get better from some belle,
who encourages my interest, all I get 's
the sort of patronizing pat they give to pets!
Women who I 'd like to take to bed
treat me like a dog and pat my head.
Beyond the pale of passion I suppose
they even let me see them with few clothes.

I hereby warn each patronizing peer
every slight on me will cost you dear.
You Lords, I loathe you all. Each time you laugh
you add a letter to your epitaph.
I'll be whispering in the Prince of Wales's ear
spoiling the prospects of some pushy peer.
Just when he thinks his fortunes start to flower

because of his proximity to power,
I'll nip the budding bloom and shred
every petal from its drooping head.

You Lords brewed all this venom and this bile.
Like a Borgia with a belladonna phial
I let some droplets fall on every joy
I choose to shrivel, sour, or destroy,
the comedian as canker, the poisonous Pierrot
making gall and vinegar out of *Veuve Cliquot*!

The spectre at your feasts who'll dump malaise
into the middle of your merriest soirées,
the baleful shadow whose black bulk blots
the sun out of all blissful, sunlit spots.
What kind of life is this I've chosen
where every generous impulse in me 's frozen?
Anything more pensive, soulful, sadder
gets jingled out by jester's bells and bladder.

(*Scotty Scott approaches the door into the house.*)

The corruption that I castigate at Court 'll
vanish once I'm through this blessed portal.

Everything that I denounce, lampoon, deplore
disappears the far side of this door.
And like a change of costume I transform
from the cruel satirist to someone warm.

I cast aside the quips and play a role
that gladdens my sad heart and cheers my soul.
I shed my loathing and my deep disdain
for that hateful world I'm forced to entertain.

The old boy cursed me.

                    Maybe I'm just mad?

(*Scotty Scott enters the house and embraces his daughter,* **Becky**.)

39

Oh lass! Oh lass! Come here and hug your dad!

More beautiful than ever. Everything all right?
Come here, lassie. Hug your old da tight.

Becky
You're a good father, Dad.

Scotty Scott
           Nay, what would I do
with no daughter in my life, no you.
I'd be lost, love.

(*Scotty Scott sighs.*)

Becky
        Such sighs! So sad!
Can't you tell me why you're sighing, Dad?
So many secrets! It's a secret why
you felt just now the need to heave that sigh,
and it's a secret who's my family.

Scotty Scott
No secret, there's no family but me.

Becky
Father's the only name for you I've had,

Scotty Scott
That's all you need to know – that I'm your dad.

Becky
In the glens before you came to claim
your daughter back, 'little orphan' was my name.

Scotty Scott
It'd've been far better if I'd left you there.

But I needed someone, someone who would care . . .
I couldna cope without.

(*Scotty Scott breaks down.*)

Becky
                    Dinna fash yersel'
only tell me what you want to tell.

Scotty Scott
Never gang outside.

Becky
                    I stay in every day
except Sundays when we go to church to pray.

Tell me about my mother.

Scotty Scott
                    Best not to stir
those perfect memories I have of her.
It'll remind me that I once had in my life
a woman, beyond all others, as a wife.
For all my misery and malformed physique
your mother loved this pitiable freak.
When she died her secret perished too:
how to give a man like me a love so true.
Her love was a flash of lightning in the night,
a ray of paradise that cast its light
right into the hell my life had been
and is again, without her on the scene.
I hope the earth lies softly on the breast
I leaned my head on once for peace and rest.
You're all I have. Thank God that I have you.

(*Scotty Scott weeps.*)

Becky

Don't cry, Dad. It tears my heart in two.
I hate to see you crying in this way.

Scotty Scott

And if you saw me laugh what would you say?

Becky

Can you no tell me what it is and share
with your daughter all this constant care.

Scotty Scott

No! No! God in Heaven be thanked
I have one haven that's still sacrosanct.
This one small corner of the universe is
where I'm free from scoffers and from curses.
Here there's innocence. Here I'm just your dad,
the holiest title a feller ever had.
Father. Father. That consecrated word
's the only honour that I'd want conferred.

Becky

Daddy! Daddy!

Scotty Scott

O where else could I find
another heart so caring and so kind?
The fiercer that I loathe the world, the more
you're all that's in it that I could adore.

What else can matter in the whole wide
repulsive world but that we're side by side.
What else need enter into heart or mind
than that we're sitting here with hands entwined.
O lass, the sole blessing Heaven above
has deigned to grant me is a daughter's love.

You're all I have where many others
have friends and relatives, wives or brothers,
vast families, a long ancestral line.
Men have many mainstays. You alone are mine.
Some people put their faith in what they own
but I put all of mine in you alone,
no gold or silver, I have Heaven to thank
you're the wealth my soul has in the bank.
Some have a God who prospers their affairs,
a God they plead to with perpetual prayers.
I'm as devotional as them, but dare I say,
you are the one I worship and obey.
Some men have their looks but I think you'll agree
Beauty has blessed you and by-passed me.

You're my family, mother, sister, daughter, wife.
You're my universe, my being, my whole life.

Everywhere else my soul 's bruised by despair.
Suppose I lost you, but that doesn't bear
thinking about a moment even. Give
your da one of those smiles that help him live.

(*Becky smiles.*)

So like your mother's. Beautiful like you.
You're so alike in many ways, you two.
She did that gesture that you're doing now,
sweeping your hand like that across your brow.
She did that too, so nothing came between
her and the innocence she kept serene.
You radiate an angel's light, so bright
I'd still behold it if I had no sight,
and, if I were blind, my sightless gaze
would feel the radiance of your healing rays.

Becky
I wish I could make you happy.

43

Scotty Scott
O you do!
I'm always happy when I'm here with you.

(*strokes her hair*)

It's so beautiful and black now is your hair.
Who'd believe it used to be quite fair?

(*Becky seizes the moment of quiet togetherness.*)

Becky
Will you no show me London when you're free.
Can we no go for a stroll, Dad, you and me?

Scotty Scott
Never! Never! Even in Mrs Bryden's care
you've never ventured out?

Becky
No! No!

Scotty Scott
Beware!

Becky
I've only been to chapel.

Scotty Scott
I dread the day
she might get followed there and led astray.
O my little lassie, let me say once more
never ever gang beyond that bolted door.
For young women like yourself the world out there
in London breathes a pestilential air.
Protect her from the blast that's spelt the doom
of many a fair but early withered bloom,
so that her father in brief moments of repose

44

may breathe the fragrance of his virgin rose.

(*Scotty Scott bursts into tears.*)

Becky
I'll no nag you to go out onto the street
or see London any more, so dinna greet!

Scotty Scott
Don't worry, lass. This greeting does me good.
Tonight I did more laughing than I should.

(*to self*)

Laughing reminds me that I should be gone.
Time to put the mask of mirth back on.

(*to Becky*)

Goodbye!

Becky
Come soon!

Scotty Scott
Aye, but I dinna ken,
since I don't control my fate, exactly when.

(*shouting to Mrs Bryden*)

Mrs Bryden! Does anybody ever spot
me coming here.

Mrs Bryden
No, absolutely not.
The street's deserted.

(*Enter HRH in the street.*)

Scotty Scott
Goodbye, dearest! *But*

are you sure that all the windows are kept shut?

Mrs Bryden

(*nodding*)

> There's a house I heard of just behind St Paul's.
> It's more secluded, and it's got high walls.
> I'll go and look tomorrow.

Becky
> Daddy, please!
> From this window here I see green trees!

Scotty Scott
> Don't stick your head out there for mercy's sake!

(*Scotty Scott thinks he hears something outside.*)

> Someone's outside!

Becky
> I come up here to take
> a breath of air, that's all.

Scotty Scott
> Beware! Beware!
> People can see you if you stand up there.

Scotty Scott

(*to Mrs Bryden*)

> You see that window there. Don't light the gas.
> People 'll see it.

Mrs Bryden
> There's very few as pass.
> You trust me, sir. Naeb'dy could get through.

Becky

(*to Scotty Scott*)

But what are you afeart of?

Scotty Scott

                Not for me, for *you*!
My little daughter!

HRH

           Scotty's daughter. Bloody hell!
Who'd've believed it? Well, well, well.

Scotty Scott

On Sundays at chapel have you ever seen
anyone following? Any gentleman, I mean.

Becky

No. Never.

Scotty Scott

        If you ever do cry out.

Mrs Bryden

Don't you worry, sir, I'll be the first to shout.

Scotty Scott

If anyone comes here, don't answer. Don't unlock
the door if you hear somebody knock.

Mrs Bryden

That door 's staying well and truly locked
even if His Royal Highness knocked.

Scotty Scott

Especially if *he* knocked! Now, goodbye.

(Exit Scotty Scott.)

Becky

I feel remorse.

Mrs Bryden
You feel remorse, pet, why?

Becky

He's so frightened for me, full of fears
and as he left his eyes filled up with tears.
Poor Dad, so good. I should've let him know
that every Sunday morning when we go
to chapel we've been followed by . . .
you know who.

Mrs Bryden
Tell your father, why?
Your father is, to put it delicately, dear.
Your father 's just a wee bit, bless us, queer.
So, you hate this young man that we see?

Becky

Hate him? Oh no, on the contrary,
Since I saw him first I fear I find
I can never get his face out of my mind.
From that first day when our two gazes met
I see his features and I can't forget.
I feel I'm his. In all my dreams I see him, but
in my dreams he's taller by a foot.
He seems strong and gentle, proud and good.
He'd look great on a horse, I know he would.

Mrs Bryden
He's charming right enough.

(HRH slips more money to Mrs Bryden.)

Becky
A man like that must be . . .

Mrs Bryden
(*holding her hand out to HRH for more money*)

O very accomplished.

Becky
Anyone could see
if they only looked into his eyes,
there's a large heart there.

Mrs Bryden
Enormous size!

(*On each word she utters she stretches out her hand to HRH.*)

Becky
Brave.

Mrs Bryden
Boldness itself.

Becky
But good.

Mrs Bryden
And *kind*.
He's extremely well-proportioned, mind –
his face, his eyes, his nose . . .

HRH
If she lists every item
and I'm going to have to pay her to recite 'em
I'm going to be cleaned out.

49

Becky
                    I love to hear
you talking about him.

Mrs Bryden
                    I know, my dear.

HRH
Fuel to the flames!

Mrs Bryden
                    Most generous of men.

HRH

(*searching his pockets*)

    O God, she's starting up her list again.

Mrs Bryden
I've thought, when I've watched him in his pew,
his blood is, maybe, tinged with noble blue.

Becky
It doesn't bother me, how blue his blood is.
I'd like him a student type who studies
here in London, sensitive and smart,
but somewhere still a country boy at heart.

Mrs Bryden
He'll be everything you hope for, I've no doubt

(*aside*)

    These modern girls are strange. Can't work 'em out.
    Full of contradictions.

(*to Becky*)

Completely mad
about you, though, is that young lad.

(Mrs Bryden holds out hand to HRH but he doesn't give her anything. Aside)

The well 's run dry. No pence. No praise.

Becky
Till Sunday comes again I count the days.
When I can't see him I feel sick at heart.
When last Sunday's service was about to start
I thought he was approaching me to speak,
my heart was racing and my legs felt weak.
Night and day he's on my mind, and he,
I'm sure, thinks of nothing else but me.
He looks so serious I'm sure he'd scorn
party-going, dancing until dawn,
and I've a feeling that there haven't been
other girls before me that he's seen.
He only thinks of me.

Mrs Bryden
On my life, that's true!

HRH

(flinging her a ring)

You give your life for me, this ring 's for you.

(Mrs Bryden withdraws to give HRH his opportunity.)

Becky
Sometimes when I'm dreaming I so wish I could
have him before me here in flesh and blood
and I'd say: I . . . I . . . I . . . I . . .

HRH

(*disclosing himself*)

Don't stutter!
'I love you' 's what those lips were made to utter.
'I adore you.' Say it go on, don't be shy

Becky

(*shouting*)

Mrs Bryden! God not here. No reply.

HRH

Just us. And that's the whole world. You and I.

Becky

Where did you come from?

HRH

Does it matter where,
Heaven or Hell, so long as I declare
'I love you'?

Becky

I pray no one caught sight of you.
Please go away. What if my father knew?

HRH

How can I go away, how can I leave
when I feel your breath, your bosom heave?
You said you loved me.

Becky

You listened?

HRH

                              Every word!
The sweetest music that I've ever heard.

Becky

You've spoken to me, now, for pity's sake, I pray,
you rest content with that, and go away.

HRH

Go away, when your fate's entwined with mine
and our destinies are like twin stars that shine
together in the selfsame patch of sky?
Go, when we're fated, you and I?

How can I go, when Heaven 's chosen me
to open a virgin's soul and make her see,
see love's our sun that's brilliant and benign.
Isn't your heart as warmed by it as mine?

The sceptres Death bestows and then withdraws,
the glory that men win themselves in wars
to make their names or capture vast terrain
to be kings of, however long they reign,
all these crowned conquerors and kings
are merely earthly transient things.
One thing, and only one thing, can transcend
this earth where everything is doomed to end,
and that one thing that we can call divine
is *love*. Be happy, Becky, you have mine.

All you have to do is turn the key
and happiness enters with your lover, me.

Love's the honey hidden in life's flower.
love 's grace supported in the arms of power.
The eagle soaring with the gentle dove,
prey and predator at peace, that's love, that's love.

It's your little hand in my hand now, like so.

(*trying to embrace her*)

Let's make love. Let's make love.

Becky

(*resisting*)

Let me go!

Mrs Bryden

(*apart*)

He's doing well, the lad.

HRH

(*aside, dropping his assumed accent*)

I think I've got her!

(*to Becky*)

Tell me you love me.

Mrs Bryden
Artful rotter.

HRH
Say it again.

Becky
You've heard me once. You know.

HRH
Then I'm a happy man . . .

Becky

I'm done for, though.

HRH

Be happy with me.

Becky

Be happy, but with who?
Tell me who you are.

Mrs Bryden

About time, too!

Becky

At least I know you're not one of those peers
my poor old father always says he fears.

HRH

God forbid! I'm just a student, nothing higher.
My name 's Gerald Murray.

Mrs Bryden

Flaming liar!

(*Duke of Peen and Sir Percival Dillon approach the outer door of the house.*)

Duke of Peen

This way! This way! Over here.

Mrs Bryden

(*listening*)

I believe
there's somebody outside.

Becky

       God, my father! Leave!

Mrs Bryden

Yes, sir, go.

HRH

       Tell me before I do,
will you love me tomorrow?

Becky

          Yes. And you?

HRH

I'll love you forever, my whole life through.

Becky

Ah, you're telling fibs like those I tell my dad.

HRH

You're the only love I've ever had.
One last kiss on those eyes before I go.

(*HRH kisses Becky's eyes.*)

Mrs Bryden

(*bustling HRH out of the door*)

       All this bleeding kissing, I don't know.

(*Exit HRH.*
  Becky opens the upper shutter to watch HRH disappear. Various nobles disguised in hoods gather near the wall protecting the house.)

Becky

I'd like to carve that loved name on my heart:
Gerald Murray.

Duke of Peen
That's the hunchback's tart.

Sir Percival Dillon
Let's see.

Lord Gossett
Back-street baggage by her looks
It's a shame you have to troll with molls of crooks.

(*Becky turns and they see her face.*)

Sir Percival Dillon
Now what do you think?

Poet Laureate
Oh yes. Oh *yes!*

Lord Gossett
Yes, she's an angel. Full of gracefulness.

Sir Percival Dillon
This is the hunchback's bit of stuff.

Lord Gordon
Sly old goat!

Poet Laureate
I think I was inspired when I wrote:

'Where Beauty is, the Beast 's not far behind
when Cupid starts confounding humankind.
Mischievous Cupid loves mismatching Man
and makes Miranda moon for Caliban.'

Duke of Peen
We didn't come here to listen to you drone

but to do a little mischief of our own.
Just like the japes we all did in the dorm,
only now it's kidnapping and chloroform,
snaffling the hunchback's little sweet.

Lord Gordon
She's just our royal master's sort of meat.

Lord Gossett
Exactly the type to catch the Prince's eye.

(*Re-enter Scotty Scott.*)

Scotty Scott
Fear 's brought me back here but I'm not sure why.

Lord Gossett
I wonder if it's right the Prince's way
of using anybody's women for his play.
How would he feel if someone did the same
to the Princess?

Scotty Scott
I know why I came.
Lord Kintyre's curse! It's made me ill at ease.

(*Hears something.*)

Who's there?

Lord Gossett

(*whispering*)

It's Scotty Scott! O what a wheeze.
We can get our two birds with one stone.
Let's do him in.

Duke of Peen
No, leave him alone.

Lord Gordon
Without the comedian around to mock
the joke would only go off at half-cock.

Lord Gossett
But the bounder 's bound to interfere.

Poet Laureate
Leave him to me. I've got a good idea.

(*to Lord Gossett*)

Quick, Gossett, give your keys to this young blade.
It needs a poet's touch, this escapade,
a poet with the sense of the dramatic.

(*to Sir Percival Dillon and Lord Gossett*)

Go into Gossett's, up into the attic,
lower the roof hoist down here to street level,
while I distract our hunchbacked Glasgow devil.

Scotty Scott

(*hearing them*)

Someone's whispering.

Poet Laureate
Scotty, is that you?

Scotty Scott
Who's that?

Poet Laureate
It's only me.

Scotty Scott
It's only who?

Poet Laureate
The Laureate.

Scotty Scott
Ah, it's so dark tonight.

Poet Laureate
The Devil's blackboard.

Scotty Scott
He must have poems to write.
But what are you here for?

Poet Laureate
You haven't guessed?
It's something HRH heard you suggest:
kidnapping Lord Gossett's wife, and so we're here
to bring about your wonderful idea.

Scotty Scott

(*to himself, relieved*)

Thank God for that.

(*then to Poet Laureate*)

What a brilliant wheeze.
How will you get in?

(*Roof hoist is lowered down as they watch.*)

Poet Laureate
This is going to please.
Our Prince. Think how chuffed he'll be
when we bring him a bit of fluff for company.

Scotty Scott

Well, if that 's the escapade you plan to do,
kidnap Lord Gossett's wife, count me in too.

Poet Laureate

We're wearing hoods.

Scotty Scott

Right, give me a hood.

(*Poet Laureate gives him a hood and Scotty Scott puts it on.*)

Now what?

Poet Laureate

Up onto the hoist.

Scotty Scott

Righto, good.

Voice of Sir Percival Dillon

(*from Lord Gossett's attic*)

Hold on, Scotty we're going to haul
you up to us.

(*The hoist begins to lift Scotty Scott into the air.*)

Scotty Scott

Steady! Steady! Or I'll fall.

(*The hoist comes to a stop with Scotty Scott suspended.
Behind him the Lords enter the house to kidnap Becky.*)

Scotty Scott

(*on hoist*)

Have you got her?

Voice 1

(*from above*)

                        Yes, Scotty, got her trussed
like a chicken for his oven of lust!

Voice 2

(*from above*)

We've got the Lady trussed up in a sack
and need to send her down on your broad back.

Scotty Scott

Aye, humps come in handy. God designed
my shape with just this escapade in mind.

(*pause*)

Why have you stopped pulling? Haul! Haul!

(*removes hood*)

What the hell? What's happened to them all?

Becky

(*from inside the sack*)

Daddy! Daddy! Daddy! Daddy!

(*Scotty Scott wriggling on the hoist removes his hood and
realizes the awful truth. He gives a great anguished cry.*)

Scotty Scott
                    FUCK!

(*He drops from the hoist.*)

Agh! Agh! The curse! The curse! It's struck!

The Gang

(*singing in receding distance*)

The Ladies! The Ladies!

Act Three: HRH

*A gentlemen's club. The usual Lords and Dukes and
HRH's hangers-on.*

Lord Gordon
Let's bring the curtain down on this charade.

Sir Percival Dillon
No, let it hit him where it hurts and really hard.
Let him realize his jests have cost him dear
and don't let him suspect his sweetheart's here.

Lord Gossett
Yes, let him search for her all night and day.
But won't the porters give the show away?

Montgomery
They've all been seen to, and they'll all deny
they saw a female person passing by.

Sir Percival Dillon
We should lead the hunchback on a wild goose-chase,
frantically searching from place to place,
mewling madly for his moll from mews to mews.
We should concoct a trail of cruel clues:
say some pimp bought her and he'd take all week
to scour the brothels and the *Poses Plastiques*,
fearing his bit of fluff's been forced to ease
drunk sailors' stiffness for a few bawbees.

Lord Gossett
Yes, let's throw him off the scent. Let's see
just how far we can prolong his agony.

Poet Laureate
I left behind a scribbled note that read:
'I've taken your little sweetheart from your bed
and put her into mine, She won't come back
We're off abroad.'

Lord Gossett
And signed it?

Poet Laureate
Spring-heeled Jack!

(*They all laugh.*)

Sir Percival Dillon
He must be going frantic.

Lord Gossett
That I long to see.

Lord Gordon
The poor devil in despair and agony
clenching his fists and teeth! He'll pay
everything he owes us in one day.

(*Enter HRH in dressing gown, laughing with Duke of Peen.*)

HRH
What've you bagged there?

Duke of Peen
Scotty's sweetheart!

HRH

Scotty's what?

Duke of Peen
Yes, believe it or believe it not
his sweetheart. Or his wife.

HRH

(*to self*)

His wife! His 'lass'!
He's a proper paterfamilias!

Duke of Peen
Would you care to look her over?

HRH

Yes, I'll say.
I'm glad of anything that comes my way.

Duke of Peen

(*to Becky still in the sack*)

Did you ever dream, my dear, that fate would bring
a private audience with your future king?
Well, that's exactly what your fate has brought,
a grace not often granted to your sort.

(*Duke of Peen opens the sack and releases Becky.*)

May I present his future Majesty,
the Prince of Wales!

Becky

(*recognizing her 'student'*)

The Prince? It canna be?

HRH

Becky!

Becky
Gerald Murray, God!

HRH
                    If my friends knew
or didn't know that they were bringing you
doesn't matter if it means that I can throw
my arms around you once again, like so.

(*HRH attempts to embrace Becky.*)

Becky
The Prince of Wales! I beg you let me go!

HRH
Let you go, the beauty I adore?
The Prince re-swears the love the student swore.
We love each other don't we, you and I?
Does being Prince of Wales disqualify
me as a lover? You didn't seem to mind
when I was a student of the serious kind.
Now because you find I'm nobly born
gives you cause for neither fear or scorn.
If I'm not a yokel, sorry. If it matters, why?

Becky
He's making fun of me. I want to die.

HRH
By turning down my offer you turn down
all the pleasures of the Court and of the Town,
parties, games and balls, and after dark
sweet nothings whispered in St. James's Park,
all the indiscretion and delight

veiled in the concealment of the night.

In this crumbling house of clay where love's the tenant
the spangles of our passion on the pennant
of life's frail fabric, flying, but threadbare,
are, nonetheless, still glittering in the air,
those spangles of our passion without which
life unravels drably stitch by stitch,
its once fine fabric faded into tatters.
I've given a lot of thought to all these matters
and the sum of wisdom is: Give God his dues.

(*aside to watching nobles*)

Then bed the beauties and imbibe the booze.

Becky
He's not like the picture that I had of him.

HRH
What did you want? Someone stammering and prim?
One of those bloodless fools who, when they woo
women, think that all they have to do
to win them over is make doleful eyes
and lay siege to beauty with their soppy sighs.

Becky
Let me go, I've been deceived.

HRH
                    Think who *we*'ll be
when millions in the Empire bow to me!
The Prince of Wales, next in succession,
power and pleasure, all in my possession.
Next in succession, that would mean
if I am to be King, then you'd be Queen.

Becky

But your wife . . .

HRH

So naive, you touch my heart.
A mistress and a wife are things apart.

Becky

A mistress is a shameful thing to be.

HRH

So proud!

Becky

My father, he will rescue me.

HRH

Your father! All I need to do is utter
the command to return him to the gutter.
Think of it. I'm destined for the Crown
And what's your father? He's a common clown.
Your father eats out of my royal hand.
Your father does whatever I command.

Becky

(*sobbing*)

You own him too.

HRH

Don't cry so. Come.

Becky

No! No!

HRH

Won't you tell me that you love me so?

Becky

No, that's over.

HRH

Becky, please don't cry.
I don't want to make you sob. I'd rather die.
What sort of cowardly monarch will I be
if women are made to weep because of me?

Becky

Tell me the truth. That it's all been a hoax.
And now you've finished with your stupid jokes
and you and your friends have had their bit of sport,
send me back to Dad. He'll be so distraught.
I want to go back home. Home is near . . . O
why should I tell you you already know.

HRH

And all this time I did believe you cared.

Becky

Now you're the Prince of Wales, I'm scared. I'm scared.

HRH

Scared? Of me?

(*attempts embrace*)

Becky
LET ME GO!

HRH

One kiss to say that I'm forgiven.

70

Becky

No!

HRH

Weird little thing.

Becky

Please let me free,

(*Becky frees herself and runs into the bedroom, locking the door behind her. HRH pulls a key from his dressing gown pocket.*)

HRH

It's just as well I've got my bedroom key.

(*HRH follows Becky into the bedroom and locks the door.*)

Lord Gordon

Hello, hello. Tell me what's happening then.

Poet Laureate

(*laughing*)

The wolf's dragged the bleating lamb into his den.
The little lamb's gone bleating baa-baa-baa
straight into the big bad wolf's boudoir.

Sir Percival Dillon

Poor old Scotty!

Duke of Peen

Sssh, he's here.

Lord Gordon

This is what we do –
Straight faces, and no smirking. Not a single clue

Poet Laureate
He only saw me there.

Duke of Peen
Ah, here he comes.
Curtain 's going up. A roll of drums.

(*sings*)

The Ladies! The Ladies!
The one who's got it made is
the one who can love 'em then flee.

Scotty Scott

(*joining in*)

There's said to be royals
who don't have the toils
and troubles the Ladies, the Ladies give me.

(*Applause.*)

All
Bravo!

Scotty Scott
Where've they hidden her?

All
Bravo!

Scotty Scott
They're all involved in it.

Lord Gossett
What ho!

Scotty Scott
O so we're Lord Cheerful are we for the day?

Lord Gossett
And how come that's your business, pray?

Scotty Scott
Only this, don't try to be amusing or
you'll end up even more a bloody bore.

(*Scotty Scott ferrets around.*)

Where've they hidden her?

(*approaches the Poet Laureate*)

                    Ah, just the man
to ask if it went well, the kidnap plan.

Poet Laureate
What plan?

Scotty Scott
          The hoods! The hoist!

Poet Laureate
                    I'm afraid
you must have dreamed this weird escapade.
The hoods? The hoist? Frankly I recommend
you drink less fizz in future, my dear friend.

(*Scotty Scott sights a handkerchief and examines it.*)

Sir Percival Dillon
He's got my handkerchief. Looking at the crest
like Sherlock Holmes pursuing an arrest.

(*to Scotty Scott*)

Do you require a magnifying glass

to find my monogram?

Scotty Scott

(*to the Duke of Peen*)

Where've they put my lass?
Gone home to sleep it off, the Prince, no doubt?

Duke of Peen

Indeed.

Scotty Scott

I'd hoped to find him still about.

Sir Percival Dillon

Home with her Royal Highness.

Lord Gordon

(*attempting a distraction*)

The poet
just told me this one do you know it?

Poet Laureate

It's from the Latin, I'm somewhat partial
to those rather raunchy epigrams of Martial:

'The gluttonous geezer Lord Pratt
grew increasingly fat,
as he doted on dinner
his wife had men in her
who doted much more on her twat.'

Lord Gossett

(*singing*)

The Ladies! The Ladies!

Scotty Scott
                Take care! Take care!

Lord Gossett
What?

Scotty Scott
      I said take care.

Lord Gossett
             And why?

Scotty Scott
                        Because he'll do
exactly the same epigram on you.

Lord Gossett
You! You!

Scotty Scott
      The strangest beast in the whole zoo
when it's really mad it cries: You! You!

(*Enter an Equerry*)

Duke of Peen
What is it?

Equerry
      Her Royal Highness sends
to be informed what HRH intends.
Will His Highness be returning, or stay late
discussing with you here affairs of state?

Duke of Peen
His Highness has retired.

Equerry
                        But the Prince
was seen with your Lordships only minutes since.

Duke of Peen
He's hunting early.

Equerry
                  Hunting? One presumes
he'd have given notice to the grooms,

Duke of Peen
He's going fishing then.

Equerry
                      What one finds odd 's
no one told the staff to pack his rods.

Duke of Peen
Dammit, then I'd better make it clear
the Prince is unavailable.

Scotty Scott
                      She's here!
She's with him!

Lord Gordon
                    He's really gone insane.
And who is she?

Scotty Scott
                    She's that wee wain
you stole from me. You! You! You.

And you, Sir Percival, were in it too.
You're all aware of what you brave men did
kidnapping a frightened little kid.

Duke of Peen

(*laughing*)

Lost your sweetheart? With your good looks you
                                        ought to
get a replacement quick.

Scotty Scott
                        I want my daughter.

All

Daughter!

Scotty Scott
                    Daughter, yes, daughter. Go on, mock.
Mock me, or are you all struck dumb with shock
that the hunchback's father of a lovely child.
Peers of the realm, wolves in the wild
have offspring of their own, so why not me?
Enough's enough. Now set my daughter free.
Yes, gentlemen, you had your little fun,
Very amusing. Very. Now it's done.
I want my daughter. Get that straight.
I know she 's here.

Poet Laureate
                    The man 's in such a state.

Scotty Scott
Was it these demons, these damned crooks of Court
kidnapped my daughter for 'a spot of sport'?
To such Court lackeys the virtue of a maid

's a mere commodity to use for trade.
When the future monarch, when the royal heir 's
a compulsive flaunter of corrupt affairs,
when the Prince's pleasure is an idle poke
virginity round this lot 's just a joke.
They let the Prince debauch their wives and girls
to end up dubbed as Knights, and Dukes, and Earls.
These chastity corrupters would all charter
their own children out to get a Garter.
Like farmers with spare acres they sublet
their spouses' pudenda for a coronet,
subject their daughters to ordeals of sex
to get some Order dangled round their necks.
Ask any puffed-up Peer: 'Was your wife whored
so her empurpled pimp got made a Lord?'
They'd see every family female flung
to the royal wolf to climb one social rung.
Is there any one of you who dare deny
the truth of what I say, or prove I lie?
You'd all allow your women to be whored
(if you haven't done it yet!) for the reward
of some pretentious title or another.

(*to Lord Bryan*)

    You, your wife!

(*to Lord Gordon*)

        Your sister!

(*to the young Sir Percival Dillon*)

           And *you*, your mother!

(*Lord Tourland goes to the sideboard and pours himself a
glass of champagne and hums a few bars of 'The Ladies,
The Ladies' as he pours.*)

Scotty Scott

(*turning on him*)

Dammit! Dammit! Dammit! Dammit! Dammit!
I ought to grab your bloody glass and ram it
down your gullet! This so-called 'noble' lot,
who claim descent as far back as year dot,
this ever so exclusive social set
who run to yards of entries in Debrett,
who claim ancestral kinship with the great
historical heroes of this ancient state,
are the same illustrious gang who stole
the daughter of this poor unhappy soul.
You're no nobles. I can hear the jeers and hoots
as mere grooms pumped your mamas like prostitutes.
You're no more grand than me. Your proper dads
were probably your father's stable lads.
You're all bastards!

Lord Gossett
You oaf!

Scotty Scott
　　　　　　　How much were you paid
to perpetrate this puerile escapade?
O, yes, he'd buy her. Making such a sale's
easy when the buyer 's Prince of Wales.

His shrunken conscience makes him show no qualms
about purchasing the pleasure of such charms.
He likes them young and beautiful, and she's
as beautiful as anything one sees.

Is a rainbow ribbon or a tinsel decoration
the going rate at Court for compensation?
If his Highness finds my daughter willing
would I get a better social billing?

79

Will his gratification make me grander –
the usual peerage for a Palace pander?
I tell you, sirs, a pettifogging title
might well be an adequate requital
for such low men as you who'd all play bawds
and lease your ladies if it made you Lords,
not *me*! If he could magically bestow
a straightened back on me I'd still say no.

You scourings of the Court, you scum
whose hearts and consciences have all gone numb,
you courtiers are all cowards who'd debauch a
woman and destroy her with your torture.

Your Lordships hear a cripple's desperate cry.
Give me back my daughter. Or I'll die.

Look at this hand. Nothing noble. Nothing royal,
just your ordinary horny hand of toil.
A navvy's hand, a serf's, for spades not swords
but enough to knock the blocks off a few Lords.
I've waited here too long. Now let's have done.
Give me back my daughter!

(*Scotty Scott makes for the door of HRH's bedroom, but is forcibly restrained.*)

                              Ten to one!
All ganged up against me!

(*Scotty Scott weeps.*)

                              Yes, these are tears.

(*Scotty Scott turns to the Poet Laureate.*)

You're a poet among these soulless peers.
Poets are meant to have compassionate hearts,
to understand the frail and take their parts.
You were born among the people just like me,

a fellow commoner for all your finery.
Tell me where she's hidden, what they've done.
She is here isn't she? You're the only one
among these heartless peers with poet's feeling.

(*No reaction from Poet Laureate.*)

Poets!

(*Scotty Scott goes down on his knees.*)

Look, your Lordships, now I'm kneeling.
to ask for your forgiveness and to tell
your Lordships that today I'm far from well.
You know me, your Lordships, I'm the bloke
who'd be the first to laugh and share the joke
when I'm myself, but not today, I'm racked
the way a feller is when he's hunchbacked.
This, you must admit, strange soberness of mine
comes from the pain that cripples my whole spine.
Poor cripples have their bad days. This is one
but never forget the days when we had fun –
'The Ladies! The Ladies!' you all sing along
when I give my rendition of our favourite song
Give me, as small return for all the smiles
I've raised, the times I've laid you in the aisles,
for all my turns and tricks and comic patter,
a sympathetic hearing in this matter.
I'm your entertainer. Look at me.
Though I'm quickly running out of repartee.

Give me back my child, who, I assume
you've hidden in the Prince of Wales's room.
My one treasured possession, gentlemen.
I beg you, beg you, give her back again

She was everything I ever had.
The one thing I took pride in, being her dad.

(*Silence.*)

> I can't make you out, you high born lot.
> Mostly you're sniggering, but when you're not
> you're absolutely silent. All right snigger
> at this pathetic, pitiable figure
> giving his own head these vicious thumps,
> pulling his hair out in colossal clumps.

(*looks at a clump of hair*)

> Hair it'll only take another night
> of life like this to turn completely white.

(*His frantic self injury is interrupted by the entrance of his daughter Becky, dishevelled and distressed, from what is HRH's bedroom.*)

Becky
Daddy! Daddy!

Scotty Scott
My little lass, it's you.

(*to Lords and Gentlemen etc.*)

> There, sirs, that's my whole family in your view.
> My angel! My house would be a house of woe
> without you. Well, your Lordships, now you know
> it was with good reason that I wept and cried
> when you see this lovely creature at my side.
> Doesn't the world seem such a better place
> when you see my daughter's innocent face?
> What father wouldn't fight with all his might
> not to let this beauty from his sight?

(*to Becky who is weeping*)

> Dinna, dinna greet. Don't be afraid.
> The whole thing was a foolish escapade.

82

But it's over now. So don't be so upset.
It gave you a proper scare though I can bet.
But they're not bad sorts. Now they can see
how much you mean to me, they'll leave us be.

(*to Peers firmly*)

Isn't that so?

(*to Becky*)

After so much bitter weeping
I'm laughing now you're back in my safe-keeping.
But you're still greeting.

Becky
You'd greet if you knew.
I'm so ashamed.

Scotty Scott
What?

Becky
I'll only talk to you.
Not in front of these.

Scotty Scott

(*the truth dawning and shouting at HRH's door*)

Not *her* as well!

Becky
Just the two of us.

Scotty Scott

(*to Peers*)

You lot, go to Hell!
And if, by the remotest chance of fate,
his Highness happens by, tell him to wait.

(*to HRH's Bodyguard*)

Tell him for his own sake, you're his bodyguard.
Tell the Prince of Wales I say he's barred.
Tell him, as his minder, not to show his face.

Duke of Peen
What a world, when fools don't know their place.

Lord Gordon
With fools, as with infants, it sometimes pays
to let them, within reason, have their ways.
We'll be in earshot if we go next door.

(*Exit all Peers except Lord Gossett who lingers.*)

Scotty Scott
Speak, lass.

(*notices Lord Gossett*)

Didn't you hear? I said *withdraw*!

Lord Gossett

(*exiting*)

Lord, the world's turned upside down
when Peers can be commanded by a clown.

Scotty Scott

(*to Becky*)

Now you can speak.

Becky
                    Daddy, earlier he came
secretly into the house . . . the shame, the shame.

(*Scotty Scott takes her in his arms.*)

Some time ago (I should have told you then)
he started following me.

(*breaks down*)

                              I'll start again.
He never spoke. At chapel I would see him too
watching me intently from his pew.

Scotty Scott
The Prince of Wales?

Becky
                    He sometimes bumped my chair
so I'd look up and see him standing there.
And then tonight he got inside and . . .

Scotty Scott
                              and his princely hand
stamped your brow with foul dishonour's brand.
His breath has poisoned the pure air you breathed.
He plucked the bloom virginity had wreathed
your brow with, lassie, my shelter and my ark,
my ray of daylight in the midst of dark.
Your soul rekindled my soul's dwindling flame.
Your dignity discreetly veiled my shame.
You were my refuge from the world's vile spite.
The angel who filled my humble home with light.
My object of devotion, my wee, wee lass
sunk in the mire of this poisonous morass.
What more can I do after such a blow.
There's nowhere lower that a man can go.

I, prostituted to the Peerage, who purvey
everything that's ribald and risqué,
to titivate corrupted titled toads
whose breeding grounds are cesspools and commodes.
Among this degradation and debauch
you were purity's inextinguishable torch.
Only that chaste daughter that I had
gave an ounce of comfort to your dad.
Me, I've been resigned to bear my lot
(it all seemed part of being Scotty Scott!)
the abasement of the hunchback, the hurt pride
that bled inside my heart until it died,
those insults, 'Quasimodo', 'Humpty', 'ape'
hurled by so-called wits to mock my shape,
I've grown used to it, and I'd prefer
such shit to shower on me. But not on her.
When you're on the gallows, then the view
of some holy shrine nearby can comfort you.
She was the shrine I've let a vandal wreck.
Now there's just the gibbet. The noose. My neck.
Just one day to blow all that apart!
Lord Kintyre's curse. That's when I felt it start.
And I lay my curse on this corrupted Court
that crushes, like a rushing Juggernaut,
woman and child, and breaks all laws
made for our guidance by a Higher Cause,
and wipes one crime out with yet another crime
and splatters everywhere with blood and slime
and flings its filth on your pure, faultless brow,
so innocent, unsullied until now.

(*to HRH's door*)

So, wherever you are skulking, Prince of Wales,
may God who weighs all justice in His scales
make you stumble where your grave already gapes
open to swallow you.

Becky

(to self)

> I pray that he escapes.
> For though the Prince of Wales has used me ill,
> somewhere he's my Gerald. And I love him still.

Lord Kintyre

(between two policemen)

> Since corruption seems to lord it over all
> and neither God nor man has heard my call
> for justice and vengeance on the one I cursed,
> I look at Britain's future and I fear the worst
> from hopeless times where monarchs like him thrive.

Scotty Scott

Not while there's justice. While I'm alive
and drawing breath in Britain I swear an oath
that someone will take vengeance for us both.

Act Four: Becky

Scotty Scott
How can you?

Becky
But I do!

Scotty Scott
                After all this time you've had
to get over this bewitchment. Mad! Mad!

Becky
I love him.

Scotty Scott
       Women's hearts! Explain
why you can love this man.

Becky
                I canna.

Scotty Scott
                     Insane.
Bizarre.

Becky
       But, Dad, you know what people say
love works in a very mysterious way.
I know he 's done me only harm and ill
but, though I don't know why, I love him still.
Dearest Father, sweetest, sweetest Dad,

88

I know you'll think me absolutely mad
but I love him so much that I'd do
anything, even die for him, as I would you.

Scotty Scott
I can forgive you, lass.

Becky
He loves *me*, I know.

Scotty Scott
Madness!

Becky
But he swore, he swore that it was so.
A handsome prince with winning words and ways,
he captivates your heart, and when he turns his gaze
on you and you look back at him, his eyes are . . .

Scotty Scott
The sheep's eyes of a wanton womaniser.
I don't want it said in future that he took
my happiness away and wasn't brought to book.

Becky
You'd forgiven him.

Scotty Scott
Not forgiven. Nor forgot.
I just needed time to hatch my plot.

Becky
But these last weeks (and please don't take offence)
I've seen you be quite friendly to the Prince.

Scotty Scott

Pretence!
You'll have your vengeance, pet.

Becky

No, Daddy, no!

Scotty Scott

Would you feel anger, lassie, if I show
that he'd betrayed you.

Becky

He wouldna. Not, the Prince!

Scotty Scott

Would seeing with your own eyes now convince
you that he did? If he didn't love you any more
would you love him?

Becky

I don't know, but he swore
he loved me yesterday.

Scotty Scott

Only yesterday!
Very well, watch this, then tell me what you say.

(*Scotty Scott and Becky look through a chink into the
pub. They see HRH in the costume of an officer.*)

Becky

There's only an officer . . .

Scotty Scott

Use your eyes . . .

(*Becky finally recognizes the 'officer' as HRH.*)

Becky

Ah! Daddy!

Scotty Scott

Have you seen through this disguise?
There's more to come I hate to tell you, lass.

(*Focus on pub interior.*)

HRH

(*to Diddicoy*)

Two things, and quick. Your sister, and a glass.

Scotty Scott

That's what he's like. The next king, by God's grace,
risking his neck in such a squalid place.
Wine goes to his head, and all the more
when there's some low pub Hebe there to pour.

HRH

(*singing*)

The Ladies! The Ladies! etc.

(*Enter Magdalena, The Diddicoy's sister, with wine and glass for HRH.*)

HRH

(*to Diddicoy who is polishing his belt*)

We soldiers always say brass gets a better shine
done out of doors. That's how I do mine.

Diddicoy

Gotcha!

(*Exit Diddicoy to where Scotty Scott and Becky are watching.*)

So what's it to be, squire? Live or die?
We've got him now.

Scotty Scott
Come back, bye and bye.

Magdalena

(*to HRH attempting to fondle her*)

Noooo!

HRH

(*imitating her accent*)

Nooooo! Nooooo's progress. Just a while ago
you pushed me away, and now it's Noooo!
A big step forward. Come here. Let's just chat.

(*Magdalena sits with HRH.*)

HRH
It's a week since I first met you at . . .
it was 'The Hercules' . . . I'd gone with . . . who?
Scotty Scott, and fell in love with you.
You're the only one I love.

Magdalena
Me, and the other twenty!
You seem like a bloke that's played around with plenty.

HRH
Yes, I'm a monster. I confess it's true.
I've been the downfall of, well, quite a few.

Magdalena

Listen to him brag. A monster among men.

HRH

Look, you invited me to this foul den
where the food 's abysmal and your 'best' Bordeaux
seems to have been slopped out of a po,
served by an ogre whose gorilla scowl
could make the finest vintages taste foul.
How does your brother dare to put his snout
next to your lovely lips' delicious pout.
But yours is the bed that I'll be sleeping in.

Magdalena

(*to self*)

Digging his own grave!

(*HRH fondles her.*)

Gerroff!

HRH

What a din!

Magdalena

(*resisting*)

Gerroff! Gerroff! Gerroff! Behave! Let go!
Didn't you hear me when I told you No.

HRH

Eat, drink, make love, behaviour on which we,
that's me and King Solomon, both agree.

Magdalena

King Solomon? By the looks of you

you've spent more time in taprooms than church-pew.

(*HRH pursues Magdalena.*)

HRH
Magdalena!

Magdalena
Tomorrow!

HRH
(*picking up chair*)

           Tomorrow, just you dare
use that word again I'll smash this chair.
Beauties don't use that word. I've had it banned.

Magdalena
(*sitting down with HRH*)

A truce?

HRH
(*taking her hand*)

      God, what a lovely hand!
Though I'm no flagellating Desert Father
I swear, O Magdalena, that I'd rather
be slapped by this hand than feel others stroke
and caress me.

Magdalena
That's just your little joke.

HRH
No! No!

Magdalena

I'm ugly.

HRH

No you're not!
You should be kinder to the charms you've got.
When love gets hold of us, we men of war
have such hot hearts they'd make Siberia thaw.

Magdalena

I bet you read that in a book.

HRH

(*aside*)

She's right!

(*to Magdalena*)

Come on! Give us a kiss.

Magdalena

Gerrrofff, you're tight.

HRH

Just drunk with love.

Magdalena

You're a devilish one,
Captain Carefree, Major Making Fun.

HRH

I'm not joking. Marry me!

Magdalena

Then cross your heart.

(*HRH crosses his heart.*)

HRH
What a dizzy and delicious little tart!

Scotty Scott
(*to Becky as they watch from outside*)

Now what do you think? Should he pay the price?

Becky
How could he? O, the liar! O my heart's like ice.
There's not an ounce of soul in that whole frame.
She's a slut, and yet he's used the same
endearments as he used on me . . .

Scotty Scott
Sssshh! The day
when he's forced to pay 's not far away.
Revenge?

Becky
Do what you want.

Scotty Scott
At last!

Becky
I'm scared.
What terrifying plan have you prepared?

Scotty Scott
It's all worked out. And don't try to restrain
your father now. It'd finish off his brain.

Go back home. You'll find clothes there. They're men's.
Take money. Lots. And head back to the glens.

Go home to Scotland and I'll join you there.
There's a wooden chest with all you need to wear,
under your mammy's picture. These last few days
I've been preparing us quick getaways.
Do as I say. Above all don't show your face
in London. Something dreadful's taking place.

Becky

Come with me, Daddy.

Scotty Scott

                    Not yet, lass. Not yet.

Becky

I'm feart.

Scotty Scott

            Dinna be feart, my pet.
Just do all I've told you. Till we meet again.

(*Exit Becky. Enter The Diddicoy.*)

Scotty Scott

You asked for twenty. Here's half now. That's ten.
You're sure he's stopping?

Diddicoy

                    Yer, it's going to pour.

Scotty Scott

Well, he won't sleep in the Palace any more.

Diddicoy

Take it easy. We're lucky with the weather.
My sister and the storm will work together.

Scotty Scott
I'll be back at midnight.

Diddicoy
     Don't bother coming back.
I'll chuck him in the Thames inside a sack.

Scotty Scott
I'd like to throw him in myself.

Diddicoy
       Fine! I'll deliver
the corpse bagged up and ready for the river.

Scotty Scott

(*counting out the ten guineas*)

Till midnight! Then you'll get the rest I owe.

The Diddicoy
This feller, what's he called?

Scotty Scott
      You should know
both what he's called and who's your hirer. I'm
called *Punishment*, and he's called *Crime*.

(*Exit Scotty Scott.*)

Diddicoy

(*checking the Heavens*)

Storm's brewing. Clouds blacking London out.
Good. Soon there won't be even dogs about.

(*Back to interior*)

Magdalena

Gerrrofffof me!

HRH

O, you tease. You tease!

Magdalena

(*singing a chorus of 'The Ladies, The Ladies'*)

But when stout lads present
(You know what is meant)
The Ladies, the Ladies they always say no.

HRH

God, your shoulders! God, your arms! So white!
A body like a goddess, yet you fight.
Tell me, Magdalena, why did God Almighty
make you such a muleish Aphrodite?

Magdalena

Enough, my brother's coming.

HRH

Just my luck!

(*Thunder, enter The Diddicoy.*)

Magdalena

That's thunder.

Diddicoy

It's going to rain like fuck.

HRH

Let it! Let it! More reason to reside
in your lodging and let the storm subside.

Magdalena

Hark at him. Talks like the royal set –
'reside' . . . 'reside'. Won't your family fret?

HRH

Family? There's no family. So no fears.
I belong to no one.

Diddicoy

(*to self*)

Music to my ears.

(*Rain pelting. Night getting blacker and blacker.*)

HRH

(*to Diddicoy*)

You, my friend, can go and lay your head
in the cellar. Or in hell. It's time for bed.

Diddicoy

Thanks.

Magdalena

(*urgently to HRH*)

Go home!

HRH

(*laughing*)

Look how it pours.
It's not fit to put a poet out of doors.

Diddicoy

(*showing Magdalena the money*)

Make him stay! Look, ten guineas, and the rest
at midnight. After.

(*to HRH*)

Sir, may I suggest
you take my humble room for your repose.

HRH

Fry in July, and freeze December. One of those?

Diddicoy

Come and look. Would your Lordship care
to view it?

HRH

Why not?

Magdalena

(*looking out of window*)

God, it's black out there.

(*Diddicoy and HRH climb up to the attic to view the
room.*)

Diddicoy

There y'are, sir, comfy bed.

HRH

Has it been
made limbless in the service of the Queen?

(*seeing broken window panes*)

And I see you like fresh air, and show

hospitality to all the winds that blow.

Goodnight!

Diddicoy
Sleep tight!

(*Exit The Diddicoy.*)

HRH
I'm feeling weary. Damn!
I'll have a nap. The girl knows where I am.

(*HRH removes his boots, lies down.*)

HRH

(*drowsily*)

The Ladies! The Ladies! And Magdalena
a lioness just waiting for her trainer!

(*HRH falls asleep.
The Diddicoy and Magdalena in the downstairs room.
She's sewing a sack. He's finishing off the bottle of wine
left by HRH. They are both thinking about the imminent
murder.*)

Magdalena
The captain's very charming.

Diddicoy
Oh, yes, I agree.
He charmed me twenty guineas for my fee.

Magdalena
Twenty? Is that all that you could get
he's worth much more.

Diddicoy

You're getting soft, my pet.
Go upstairs. Check he's asleep. And fetch
his sword downstairs.

(*Magdalena goes up into the loft.*
Enter, outside in the storm, Becky, dressed in the riding
clothes of a man, boots with spurs etc.
Magdalena looks at the sleeping HRH.)

Magdalena

He's asleep, poor wretch.
It's really such a shame. Poor lad! Poor lad!

(*Magdalena comes down from the attic with HRH's*
sword.)

Becky

(*outside*)

This is so frightening. I must be mad.

He's spending the night here. God don't let
whatever's going to happen happen yet.
I'm sorry, Daddy, sorry. I'm afraid
I've come back here. I've disobeyed.
Before I used to live quite unaware
of the great, wide world and all its care.
Now, from a secluded life, I'm hurled
into the darkest corner of the world,
my happiness, well-being, my virginity,
demolished into dust and bleak debris.
Do all love's fervent, bright flambeaux
only leave behind cold ash and woe?
It's like a funeral. Hard to believe
that soot and ash are all such blazes leave.

(*Thunder.*)

Such noise, such thunderclaps! It makes me wonder
if it doesn't come from my heart, this violent thunder.
What am I doing in this hellish night?
My own shadow used to make me jump with fright.
But all the desperation and despair
that makes wronged women daring makes me dare.

(*Sees light in house.*)

What's going on? This place makes my heart chilled.
I hope to God that no one's getting killed.

(*Inside hovel.*)

Diddicoy
What weather!

Magdalena
Rain and thunder.

Diddicoy
                              Wedlock in the sky,
the husband's shouting makes his missus cry.

Becky
(*outside*)

If my father only knew I'm doing this.

(*Inside hovel.*)

Magdalena
Brother!

Becky
(*listening at crevice*)

They're talking.

Diddicoy
Yeh, what is it, sis?

Magdalena
Know what I'm thinking?

Diddicoy
No.

Magdalena
Try guessing, then.
Don't let's kill him. He's a Greek god among men,
sleeping like a baby, the handsome lad upstairs.
And he really fancies me. Or so he swears.
Don't let's kill him.

Becky

(*outside listening*)

God!

Diddicoy
Sew that sack, and quick.
Once my razor's done his little trick,
your Greek god goes in it. With this stone.
And splash into the Thames. So get it sewn.

Magdalena
But . . .

Diddicoy
Not your business! If I listened to your din
none of the fellers 'd ever get done in.
So sew the flaming sack.

Becky

(*outside*)

It's like I gaze
straight into hell's most horrifying blaze.

Magdalena
All right, but let's talk.

Diddicoy
Why not?

Magdalena
Do you detest
the captain?

Diddicoy
No, the military are best.
We share the same profession, he and I.

Magdalena
And you're prepared to let that young man die,
an officer with gentleman's finesse
for that ugly devil with a back bent like an S?

Diddicoy
Look, I get ten guineas to dispose
of him from the hunchback. Then once he knows
the corpse in the sack is in the river
I get another ten, so we'll deliver.

Magdalena
But wouldn't it be the same thing if you jump
the hideous little feller with the hump
and kill him for the money?

Becky

(*outside*)

Daddy!

Magdalena

(*insisting*)

Yes, it would!

Diddicoy

I don't go shedding anybody's blood.
I'm sorry but it goes against my trade
to kill a client, specially one what's paid.

Magdalena

So put a log inside the sack instead.
It's dark enough to pass for someone dead.

Diddicoy

Nah, a log 'd be no bloody good.
Who'd take it for a stiff, a bit of wood?
It's far too rigid, and it feels too rough.
It isn't lifelike. Doesn't bend enough.

Becky

(*outside*)

This rain's so cold. I'm going to freeze.

Magdalena

Pity him.

Diddicoy

Get lost!

Magdalena
Brother, brother, please!

Diddicoy
Ssshh! He's got to die, so shut it, see.

Magdalena
I'll wake him up and say he's gotta flee.

Becky

(*outside*)

Good for you!

Diddicoy
And what about my pay?

Magdalena
Too bad.

Diddicoy
Magdalena, let me have my way,
and do the thing that I've been paid to do.

Magdalena

(*blocking the staircase*)

I want to save him. I won't let you through.

(*They struggle.*)

Diddicoy
Look, it's nearly midnight, and the hunchback's due.
If somebody, anybody, comes before
asking for shelter, knocking at the door,
I'll kill him instead, and put him in the sack
and you can have your Greek god feller back.

Magdalena
O very generous, brother, Ta!
Where the hell d'ya think these travellers are?

Diddicoy
Sorry, it's the best that I can do.

Magdalena
So late.

Becky

(*outside*)

Is something drawing me towards that fate?
If I crossed the threshold I could save
the beast I'm still in love with from the grave.
I'm too young to die. My heart keeps saying: *knock*!

Magdalena
In such a storm and nearly 12 o'clock
nobody's coming.

Diddicoy
If they don't, he's dead.

Becky

(*outside*)

I should call the watch. They're all in bed.
But if this pair blabs, things could be bad –
plotting to kill the Prince – for my poor Dad.
I don't want to die. I've better things to do.
Daddy, I want to live to comfort you.
I'm only sixteen! That's too young to feel
my neck slit open by the cut-throat's steel.

(*A clock begins to strike 11.45 p.m.*)

Diddicoy
That's it, a quarter to. No one 'll show
with only fifteen minutes left to go.
I've got to get a move on. Time's a-flying.

Magdalena
(*weeping*)

Wait, just a bit.

Becky
(*outside*)

She's crying. Crying!
And I'm doing nothing, when I could
save the Prince by shedding my own blood.
And since he doesn't love me any more
what am I still scared of dying for?
So horrible, to be stabbed. To gasp. To bleed.

Diddicoy
No more waiting. I've got to do the deed.

Becky
(*outside*)

What's dying like? If only you could know
what it feels like when they strike the blow.
If only it were painless. But I'm afraid
of seeing it flash towards me, the sharp blade.

(*Magdalena still tries to prevent The Diddicoy from going upstairs to kill HRH.*)

Diddicoy
No one's coming now. I've just got time
to do him in before the midnight chime.

Becky
(*outside*)

I'm frozen.

(*decides*)

Right! To die as cold as this.

(*Becky knocks on the door of the hovel.*)

Magdalena
Someone's knocking!

Diddicoy
No, it's loose slates, sis.

Magdalena
Someone's knocking!

Diddicoy
That's strange.

Magdalena
(*calling out*)

Who's there?

(*to Diddicoy*)

A lad!

Becky
(*outside*)

Is there a night's shelter to be had?

Diddicoy
You're going to rest far longer than a night!

Magdalena
You've come to the best place here, all right.
This is the best place that you could have chosen.

Becky
Let me in. I'm really frozen. Frozen!

Diddicoy
Wait! Wait! Don't let him in just yet.
I need to give my friend a little whet.

(*Diddicoy sharpens his razor.*)

Becky
He's sharpening his razor. I can hear it scrape.
There's no going back. There's no escape.

Magdalena
Poor young man. He's knocking on his tomb.

Becky
Am I going to die? O God to whom
I'm journeying I beg you to forgive
the Prince my dying will allow to live.

Forgive the Prince of Wales and bless his reign.
And forgive these criminals by whom I'm slain.
Forgive the hired murderer who slays a
child of sixteen with a sharpened razor.
The slaughtered sacrificial lamb 'll lay her
wrecked life down for her betrayer.

God bless the Prince of Wales, long may he reign.

May his prosperity wax and never wane.
If he's happier forgetting, let
him never think of me and totally forget.
To give him life I sacrifice my own.
Let him wield power wisely on the throne.

The razor's sharp by now.

Magdalena

(*to Diddicoy*)

Hurry, he won't stay.

(*Diddicoy tests the blade.*)

Diddicoy

Good!

(*to Magdalena*)

Don't open till I say.

Becky

I can hear them.

Magdalena

Just give me the nod.

(*After a pause The Diddicoy nods. Magdalena opens the door and Becky enters.*)

Becky

Kill me, but don't hurt me. God, O God

Magdalena

(*shouting*)

Do it! Do it!

Becky
The sister's just as bad.
God forgive them. And you forgive me, Dad.

(*The razor flashes down.*)

Act Five: Scotty

The same riverside hovel as for Act Four.
  Enter Scotty Scott.

Scotty Scott
Revenge at last! The blow that's just been struck 's
been worth this anxious month on tenterhooks.
I've worn my mask as ever and kept in
the agony behind the comic's grin.

(*Goes up to the door of hovel/tavern.*)

To know that vengeance has been duly dealt
with concrete proof that can be touched and felt.
The very door, and the moment's almost due
for the royal corpse to be 'escorted' through.

(*Thunder.*)

What a night! Perfect for such dark doings though –
a storm in Heaven, murder here below.

I feel gigantic! Like those gods who hurled
thunderbolts of wrath down on the world.
I've killed the future king, one who commands
the Empire that extends to distant lands,
who'd lord it over Sikh and Hottentot,
stopped dead in his tracks by Scotty Scott

Once I've pulled away this princely prop
where will the shock waves and the tremor stop?
It'll make all Europe and the Empire shake
at the coming of some cataclysmic quake.

Once a Windsor's dumped into the Thames
all dynasties look to their diadems.
Rulers reading the sensational reports
want extra sentries mounted round their Courts.
Every ruler on his rocking throne
will look at this death here and fear his own.
This act could fan the coals and goad
those with a grievance down revenge's road,
fuel disaffection to a fever pitch
against all royals and the idle rich.
The rebellion starts here with Scotty Scott.
One day they'll raise his statue on this spot.

Questioning the Earth, our Lord Creator
cries 'What vast volcano bursts its crater?
What force is so mighty? Who? Or what?'
And the Earth gives answer 'Scotty Scott!'
Shudder at the name of Scotty Scott, a
force to make the British Empire totter!

(*Dying thunder. Midnight chimes.*)

Midnight!

(*Scotty Scott knocks at the door.*)

Diddicoy
(*from inside*)

Who's there?

Scotty Scott
Me!

Diddicoy
Wait!

Scotty Scott
Hurry!

Diddicoy
                              Wait, I said.

(*Pause. Then a half-door opens and Diddicoy pushes a
sack out through it.*)

Diddicoy
He's heavy. Give me a hand and take his head.
He's in the sack, your man.

Scotty Scott
                              Joy makes me cry.
Give me a light.

Diddicoy
No! No!

Scotty Scott
                              But why?

Diddicoy
There's Peelers who patrol round here at night,
and you've made noise enough. No light. *No* light.
The money!

(*Scotty Scott gives The Diddicoy ten more guineas.*)

Scotty Scott
Here! Such happiness in hate.

Diddicoy
Let's dump him in the river now. It's late.

Scotty Scott
I can manage.

The Diddicoy
Two makes it quicker, though.

117

Scotty Scott

The lightest load 's the corpse of a loathed foe.

The Diddicoy

Do as you like then, squire, but take care.
Don't throw the sack from here. It's better there.
It's deeper. And be quick. I'll sling my hook.

(*Exit The Diddicoy back into the hovel.*)

Scotty Scott

How I long to look. How I long to look.
He's in there. In the sack. It's true. It's true
There's his 'blue' blood seeping through.

Here's the comic, and there's the future king.
Tell me now which one 's the underling.
The elitest of Establishment elite
who I can trample now beneath my feet.
The bloody great Panjandrum but
prostrated underneath my booted foot.
One who'd hold an Empire underneath his sway
is Emperor of one wet sack today.
The Prince of Wales, so powerful, so proud,
the Thames his sepulchre, a sack his shroud.
And who brought this about? I'm that man of action
to whom this death brings endless satisfaction.
When the *Times* devotes its front page to the deed
the people won't believe the news they read.
I'll go down in history, renowned
for removing from the world one almost crowned,
who would have had the world beneath his sway,
this would-be king it took a fool to slay.
I'll go down in history, a name
to be scared of in the Hall of Fame.
This almost mighty monarch owes his mighty fall
to a common midget from the Music Hall,

the buffoon who bounded from the humble boards
to be the latest terror in Tussaud's.
His power would have reached Earth's distant corners
with his sycophantic Court of servile fawners,
with his wealth, his gold, his jewels and his gems,
dumped like an abortion in the Thames.

Tomorrow there'll be posters everywhere
and proclamations made in every square
offering rewards regardless of the cost
for news of the Prince of Wales who's lost.
All that princely, pleasure-bent panache
gone like a puff of smoke.

(*Flash of lightning.*)

                              Or lightning flash!
Marvellous! O my poor ill-treated lass
the punishment I promised 's come to pass.
I needed his blood. Badly. A bit of gold
in the right hands. Hey presto! And behold!

(*Savagely at the sack.*)

Bloody villain! Can you hear me in your sack?
You took my daughter and you sent her back
dishonoured, and she, my lassie, 's worth
all the royal crowns there are on earth.
Are you listening? The world's turned upside down.
It's me who's commanding now, the common clown.
Because of all the jokes that I still cracked
you never saw beneath the comic act,
blind to the anger burning underneath,
you thought a father's wrath had blunted teeth.
In this unbalanced contest you began
between a future king and common man,
between the weak and strong, the victory's gone
to one no punter would put money on.

I joined the courtiers' queue and stood in line
to lick your royal boots, now you lick mine.

(*kicks the sack*)

Are you listening? It's me, your Highness, me,
the Glagow comic, the deformity
your snapping fingers often brought to heel.
You're lying at my feet. How does it feel?
Once the spirit of revenge invades our breasts
it's sleeplessly alert and never rests.
The pygmy's now a giant, the servile flea 's
muscled and menacing like Hercules.
When the slave draws vengeance from its sheath
the kitten roars and shows its tiger's teeth.
And the comic with his sycophantic cracks
becomes the executioner with bloodied axe.

I'm glad you're dead, but wish you could have heard
everything I've said, and this, my parting word:
'I loathe you, Prince of Wales.' Your days as rover,
rake and roué are, regretfully, now over.
Depending on the tide, your Highness might resort
either to the Tower or to Hampton Court.

Come on, Prince of Wales, into the drink.
One pleasure 's left. To watch your body sink.

(*Scotty Scott lifts the sack, and is about to push it into
the Thames, when he hears the voice of HRH singing a
chorus of 'The Ladies, The Ladies'.*)

Scotty Scott

That voice! That voice! That voice! This eery night
's just playing tricks on me. Let me get light.

The Voice of HRH

The Ladies! The Ladies!

Scotty Scott

Hell and damnation! He's got away!
Somebody's gone and robbed me of my prey.
Betrayed! Cheated!

(*shouts at tavern/hovel*)

Bloody Diddicoy!

(*Looks at window to see if he can climb in.*)

Too high!
So what have they used to trick me by?
Some poor soul. I'm scared. It's a corpse all right.
Not a lamp lit anywhere. I need the sky
to send another flash.

(*Lightning flash and he sees Becky in the sack.*)

No! No! How? Why?

My wee lassie! Becky! God, it's wet, my hand.
It's blood . . . But whose? My lassie's. I don't understand.
It's an hallucination. No! No! No!
I sent you to Scotland. I saw you go.

God, I beg you, let this nightmare pass.

(*Lightning flash.*)

It's her! It's her! My poor wee lass!

Becky

(*coming to*)

Where am I?

Scotty Scott

Lassie, all I've ever had
on earth, don't you know my voice. It's Dad.
What have they done to you, those fiends from hell?

Where are you wounded, lassie? I can't tell.
I'm scared to touch you.

Becky
                    All I know
's I saw the razor flash.

Scotty Scott
                    Who struck the blow?

Becky
Everything's my fault. I told a lie.
I loved him too much. Now I'll die.

Scotty Scott
Fate's got me underfoot, my daughter caught
under my vengeance's relentless Juggernaut.
How did they come to do it, lass. Explain.

Becky
Don't make me, Daddy. I'm in too much pain.

Scotty Scott
But I'm losing you, and don't know why.

Becky
Dad, I'm choking!

Scotty Scott
                    Please don't die. Don't die.
Help, somebody! Anybody! Anybody there?
Is my daughter going to die and no one care?
There's the ferry bell there on the wall.
Lassie, let me go a second, while I call
for help. There's a bell there I could ring.
You dinna want me to. How hard you cling.

Help! Help! God, it's like a graveyard here.
Don't die, lassie. Don't die, my dear, my dear.
I'll be totally deserted if you go.
My darling daughter. Don't die. Don't.

Becky

(*in pain*)

Oh! Oh!

Scotty Scott
Is my arm the problem? I'll move it. There.
Is that better? O keep on drawing air
until help comes. Don't die. Don't die.

Becky
Daddy, I'm so sorry. Ah! Goodbye!

(*Becky dies. Scotty Scott rings the ferry bell madly.*)

Scotty Scott
Help! Help!
            Oh God, what can you mean
demanding my daughter now? She's just sixteen.
O lass, don't leave your Daddy on his own,
never to hear again your tender tone.

(*People begin to assemble with torches and lanterns. As
they enter HRH's Bodyguard ushers HRH away from the
scene.*)

Heaven was pitiless when it gave me you.
Why weren't you taken long before I knew
the beauty of your spirit. It's so cruel
being allowed to know I had a jewel.
Why didn't you die sooner, like the day
the other children hurt you in their play?
O lassie! Lass!

Woman

(*listening*)

He breaks your heart in two.

Scotty Scott

(*aware of the gathering people*)

You lot took your time.

(*to a man dressed like a cabbie*)

You, you great clod, you!
Have you got a carriage?

Carter

Yes, but there's no need for that.

Scotty Scott

Put my head under the wheels and crush it flat.

(*Scotty goes back to Becky.*)

Oh lassie!

Spectator

She's been murdered, the young kid.
Her father's really gone and flipped his lid.
We should separate them.

(*They try.*)

Scotty Scott

No, leave me alone.
I want to be with her, close to her, my own.

(*to Woman who is weeping.*)

You're weeping. You've got a tender heart.
Don't let those people force us two apart.

Down on your knees, you wretch. You should have died
when she died, by your daughter's side.

(*sobs*)

Woman
You'll have to be a good bit calmer, sir,
or they'll come again and pull you off of her.

Scotty Scott
No! No! Look there. Look, I believe
she's breathing. I just felt her bosom heave.
Go fetch help, and let my daughter lie
in her father's arms. No, she won't die.
God wouldn't want it. God must surely know
she's all I care for on this earth below.

When you're mis-shapen people shun
your company, but not this little one.
She loves me. When I'm scorned, she cries.
She supports me. She can sympathize.
She was my comfort always. She is now.
Give me a handkerchief to wipe her brow.

(*He wipes Becky's brow.*)

To be so beautiful, and yet so dead.
Look at her mouth, her lips, so rosy red.

When she was two years old, her toddler's hair
not black like it is now, was light and fair.
When she was a baby this is how
I'd hold her to my heart like I do now.

She'd open her angelic eyes and see
not a hump-backed monster but her Daddy, me.
She smiled at me. She loved me as I am.
I'd kiss her small sweet hands, poor little lamb.
She isn't dead. Oh no, she's still alive

She may have fainted but she'll soon revive.
She looked like this before, and then
opened her eyes. She will, she will again.

Now you see I'm reasonable and calm.
You see I'm doing no one any harm.
I'm hurting nobody, so let me be.
My daughter 's in my arms and safe with me.

(*looking at Becky in his arms.*)

Not a wrinkle on her brow. Not a trace
of all that agony on her sweet face.
Her hands were cold. She'd been out in the storm.
I put my hands round hers and made them warm.
Feel them!

Second Woman
Here's a doctor, sir!

Scotty Scott
I won't stop you, doctor. Look at her.
She's fainted, hasn't she?

(*The Doctor examines Becky briefly then rises.*)

Doctor
It's no good.
She choked to death, she choked on her own blood.

Scotty Scott
I brought this dreadful happening to pass.
It was me, her Dad, who murdered my wee lass.

(*Police enter to arrest him. To audience*)

Laugh! This is the best laugh of the night.
Laugh at how I've murdered my own wee mite.